How to
MANAGE
YOURSELF
and
OTHERS

Francis Szarejko

Logos International
Plainfield, New Jersey

ACKNOWLEDGMENTS

The Scripture quotations in this publication are from the Revised Standard Version of the Bible, copyrighted 1946, 1952, © 1971, 1973 by the Division of Christian Education of the National Council of the Churches of Christ in the U.S.A., and used by permission.

Verses marked TLB are taken from The Living Bible, copyright © 1971 by Tyndale House Publishers, Wheaton, Ill. Used by permission.

We gratefully acknowledge the use of excerpts from the following copyrighted material:

Copyright © 1971 by Arlington House, New Rochelle, New York. Taken from *The Permissive Society* by Boris Sokoloff, M.D., Ph.D. Used with permission. All rights reserved.

Christianity Today for excerpt from "The Cultural Seduction of the Church" by Brendan F.J. Furnish, June 18, 1976. Copyright © 1976.

Excerpts from Thomas à Kempis, *The Imitation of Christ* edited by Harold Gardiner, S.J. Copyright © 1955 by Doubleday & Company, Inc. Used by permission of the publisher.

CONTENTS

DEDICATION

To Marsha, Tammy, Kathy and John Michael with whom the Lord has so abundantly blessed me. Without their patience, encouragement, interruptions and sticky kisses this book could not have been written.

INTRODUCTION

WHY THIS BOOK?

Go therefore and make disciples of all nations, baptizing them in the name of the Father and of the Son and of the Holy Spirit, teaching them to observe all that I have commanded you; and lo, I am with you always, to the close of the age. (Matt. 28:19-20)

Tend the flock of God that is your charge, not by constraint but willingly, not for shameful gain but eagerly, not as domineering over those in your charge but being examples to the flock. (1 Pet. 5:2-3)

The above quotations from Scripture lay the foundation for all that follows in this book. From the Gospel of Matthew we have the command of Christ to take the message of salvation to all the world. That means to all men, to all races, to all nations and to all professions. For this reason, the book was written that those who practice the profession of management in an increasingly secular and organization-dominated world might better understand how to be disciples of the Lord Jesus Christ.

The quotation from 1 Peter refers to a special calling of some disciples—that of a shepherd. The men and women who find themselves established in positions of authority over others are more than managers. Whether they want to recognize it or not, they have been assigned pastoral responsibility for those who work for them. The role of the shepherd carries with it its own unique responsibilities, trials and rewards. This book seeks to make the reader aware of the pastoral nature of management.

The number of those who are managers of others grows daily as new organizations are born and more mature ones expand. As the problems of management become more complex, managers are increasingly searching for something to fill the emptiness that management training, technologies and philosophies cannot fill. Success in the organization through the achievement of a high position or receiving a substantial salary and benefits, cannot fill that void that causes one to reach out to something, to someone, to relieve the loneliness of the inner person. Nothing in management education teaches us how to help ourselves spiritually or how to meet the spiritual needs of our employees. Jesus alone can fill that empty space. If you have such a need and want Him with you, He will walk the halls and sit in the board meetings of whatever corporation, whatever government agency, whatever organization employs you.

This book was written to provide the reader with an introduction to personal and professional management based on teachings found in the Scripture. It will help him apply the principles of Christian living to his profession and personal life. The reader will find advice on how to be more than a manager, how to also be a minister to his staff—a relationship that entails significantly more than the secular understanding of management would allow.

This book is about how one can be both a disciple of Jesus Christ and a manager of others in a modern organization. It shows the individual how to be effective in his relationships with others. Being a disciple is never an easy task but the very nature of the manager's job makes this walk even more difficult. The manager, because he is responsible for others and the monetary resources under his control, finds himself struggling to follow the Lord in difficult and delicate situations. If he is to be a disciple, the manager must learn how to be in the world but remain apart from it while effectively performing his job at the same time.

To reach this goal, we will attempt to do three things to help us learn to be effective managers. First, we will show that the teachings of the Bible are applicable to the practice of management. Second, a theory of management will be developed that is based on God's, rather than man's, wisdom. Finally, on the basis of Scripture, a framework is provided to assist managers in carrying out their pastoral responsibilities. This will be aimed at helping the reader learn to walk more closely to Jesus, and come to an understanding of management as a ministry. It is hoped that this framework, while drawing the reader into a deeper relationship with Christ, will help each to learn how to better work with and for other people.

A Personal Note

This is a study in building effective relationships with others. It is designed for leaders and for all who want to learn skills of personal and professional management. We emphasize the important topics of active listening, genuineness, empathy, decision making and spiritual growth. Although the book is primarily written for management professionals, it contains practical suggestions for every individual who wants to learn how to develop meaningful interpersonal relationships.

How to MANAGE YOURSELF and OTHERS

Francis Szarejko

PART I

IS CHRIST NEEDED
IN MANAGEMENT?

1

Is Christianity Compatible with Management?

And whatever you do, in word or deed, do everything in the name of the Lord Jesus, giving thanks to God the Father through him. (Col. 3:17)

Natural man likes to very carefully divide the sacred from the secular. Under the influence of the powers of darkness our society tries to confine the teachings of Christ to church buildings, priests, ministers and Sundays. Many are quick to point out that "God has His place, but it's not in the 'real' world."

Most managers work in such an environment. If he is a Christian, the professional manager must understand the place of his faith in this part of his life. He must address and answer the question: "Are the teachings of Christ compatible with a secular pursuit such as management?"

Those whose faith is narrow, who pay only lip service to the Word of God, whose personal contact with Christ is limited to an occasional prayer, will answer that it is not. However, for those who desire to live according to God's Word, who seek to be disciples of the Lord Jesus, the answer is clear: "Do *everything* in the name of the Lord

Jesus" (Col. 3:17 author's italics).

Loss of Faith

If we desire to be obedient to God we will "seek first his kingdom and his righteousness" (Matt. 6:33). This means we will place God first and let Him guide us in every area of our lives. If a manager desires to do the will of God he must seek the Father's direction in each managerial action that he takes.

Man often disagrees with God and is disobedient to His commands. Despite the directive to the contrary, Adam chose to eat the forbidden fruit in order to fulfill his desire to possess the knowledge that he thought would make him like God (Gen. 3). Adam lacked the faith to live as his Creator had instructed and sinned by pridefully trying to become equal with God.

Men have continued to follow Adam's example and put themselves in the place of God, believing they are wise and understanding in and of themselves. Without question, man's understanding of his environment and himself has grown over the centuries. With modern science and technology, our storehouse of learning and information has continued to expand at a phenomenal rate. With this sort of advance, reliance on God and faith in His provision has decreased as rapidly as man's knowledge has increased. As man depends more on his own wisdom he desires less to possess true wisdom because he has lost faith.

As he turns his back on God, man closes the door to wisdom, for "The fear of the Lord is the beginning of knowledge" (Prov. 1:7), and "For the Lord gives wisdom; from his mouth come knowledge and understanding" (Prov. 2:6).

Man's Thought Systems

The development of modern philosophical thought reflects this movement away from God and toward human intellect. While most philosophers are not widely read, the society and culture in which the masses of people grow, learn and live, is profoundly affected when the basic tenets of this or that philosophical system are applied to all areas of human learning and, most devastatingly, to education.

Systems of thought such as those grounded by Kant, Hegel and Kierkegaard have steadily influenced the development of theologies which deny the existence of the God of the Bible. While some postulate the existence of a god or force, they reduce his role to that of an uninterested observer of mankind.

These philosophies further depend on man's reasoning power by ignoring the revelation of God through the Bible in the formulation of theories that answer the basic questions about man's existence, purpose and future.

In a recent article, Brendan Furnish has explained how man-oriented thought systems have affected the viewpoint of our society as a whole, including the institutional church. He writes:

> Using this approach [i.e. that of nineteenth-century humanism], modern man was able to redefine this conception of both God and himself. Man could be viewed entirely as a product of his environment, and therefore as a being who could largely determine his own destiny. Man had within himself the power to be perfect. He could become godlike. Finally, this knowledge system was solidified by the evolutionists'

explanation of human origins which freed man from acknowledging any sort of creator. Creation was only an accident.[1]

Here we must recognize a parallel with the fall of man as recorded in Genesis as the above statement succinctly describes a modern version of man's original sin.

Influenced by these speculations, all fields of human knowledge have migrated away from the truth. The move has been from the Bible, unchangeable since its first words were inspired by the Holy Spirit, to volumes of scholarly works which vary widely in theory and are disproved and replaced on library shelves with new opinions almost as quickly as they can be written and printed. God's wisdom is unchanging and eternal. Man's wisdom is fluctuating and temporary. Yet, man chooses to trust himself.

It was under the influence of this transitory wisdom that Freud developed his theories of human psychology. These theories revolve around the satisfaction of man's pleasures beginning and ending with sex. "Freud's doctrines, and particularly his ethics, are the product of his concept of the human race. There is no purpose in man's existence. There is no goal in mankind's presence on earth. There is no God . . . and if this is so, all is permitted."[2]

Freud's psychology has made an impact on management theory. Most of the behavioral science on which approaches to management have been formulated can trace its ancestry to the Viennese doctor. As a result, these "enlightened" theories place much stress on the role of management to meet the physical, social, emotional and psychological needs of their employees while ignoring the

[1]Brendan F.J. Furnish, "The Cultural Seduction of the Church," *Christianity Today*, June 18, 1976.
[2]Boris Sokoloff, *The Permissive Society* (Arlington House: New Rochelle, N.Y., 1971) quoted in Hal Lindsey, *Satan Is Alive And Well On Planet Earth* (Zondervan Publishing House: Grand Rapids, Mich., 1972), p. 93.

spiritual part of the person. They fail to recognize and to minister to the whole man because they reject the understanding which can only be given by God.

The following quotation from Bob Mumford is also applicable to those who are trained in management:

> Many people who have graduate degrees in psychology or engineering or medicine trust God in the 'religious' areas of their life, that is, in going to church on Sunday, making moral decisions about lying or cheating, or even tithing their money. But, when it comes to their own specialty—psychology, engineering, medicine—pride causes them to reject God's guidance.[3]

Rationalization and Self-Deception

This separation of the sacred from the secular has caused the building of an environment conducive to man's rationalization of leaving God out of most of his life, if not all of it. However, this environment is constructed on the false premise that God does not exist or is at least not interested. Scripture asserts that God has revealed himself to all. When we do not recognize Him it is because we choose not to, we have lied to ourselves. "For what can be known about God is plain to them [the ungodly], because God has shown it to them. Ever since the creation of the world his invisible nature, namely, his eternal power and deity, has been clearly perceived in the things that have been made. So they are without excuse" (Rom. 1:19-20).

When a man has no excuse for his actions, he must either recognize his error or rationalize it until it becomes, in his mind, the truth. The first reaction of a man I know

[3]Bob Mumford, *Take Another Look At Guidance* (Logos International: Plainfield, N.J., 1971), p. 63.

7

who received a substantial overpayment from his employer was that he would return the extra money. But, he gradually began to justify keeping it because of the extra hours he had worked without pay. If the Holy Spirit had not revealed his error to him, and he was not spiritually aware enough to realize that the Lord was speaking to him, he would have convinced himself that it was not wrong to keep the money.

We do the same thing when we try to justify our leaving God in the church building and visiting Him on Sunday. Every excuse we have for "keeping God in His place" is based on a self-deception that is facilitated by a lack of faith in God and a rejection of the truth of His Word.

A purpose of this book is to show that God is interested in every part of our lives, specifically the realm of management, and that Jesus Christ must be Lord of everything we do. Before we can go on to discuss why this is so we must consider some popular objections to our viewpoint and examine them in the light of the Scripture. The remainder of this chapter, then, seeks to put aside some of the objections to placing God first in every part of our lives.

Objection 1–Christ's Teaching Is Outdated.
It is not uncommon to hear someone complain that Jesus founded His church nearly 2,000 years ago and the world has changed so much since He walked upon it that His teachings are only relevant to a small portion of man's life.

If it was the nature of Christ to change as man's understanding of the world has changed through the last twenty centuries then this complaint would be valid. But God's Word tells us that Jesus is unchangeable. "Jesus Christ is the same yesterday and today and forever"

(Heb. 13:8). He is still with us as He was at the beginning of time and He has not changed any of the principles by which we must live to be called children of God. He told us that His words are eternal, "Heaven and earth will pass away, but my words will not pass away" (Mark 13:31), and to be His disciples we are still called to abide by this word.

Jesus invites all men to give up their lives for Him that He may dwell in them and lead them. Our culture has ignored this and the results are seen in rising crime rates, increased drug abuse, a loss of respect for those in authority, and a plague of broken families, to select a few of our problems. The teachings of Christ show us how to live with one another and how to cope with the trials of life. Instruction in this is sadly lacking today and the principles of Christian living remain the answer. But, to be effective, they must be applied to every aspect of a person's life.

For twenty-six years I thought I knew Christ but the only places I gave Him in my life were in church on occasional Sundays, in rare prayers and in times of serious need. When I took my first management position I was determined to become a success. I was well on my way to achieving my goal by worldly standards when I realized and admitted that I was empty inside.

During this time the people on my staff were only tools to be used in accomplishing objectives. I recognized that they had needs but cared only about meeting those I thought were necessary to the performance of the job. Whenever a problem arose I worried my way through it and, if I could not solve it, I was usually able to gloss it over or push it aside. It was not long before the pressures of striving for success began to gnaw at me.

Then, I met Jesus in His fullness and was baptized in

the Holy Spirit. My work took on a different light and I saw the people with whom I worked through a new pair of eyes.

Problems are still part of the job but now I know that Jesus is always with me. People are not tools for my use and I recognize that their needs go beyond that of basic physical necessities. I now make every effort to bring Jesus' love into the office. The tension, the worries, the striving that was so much a part of my life is now gone. The job is done better because I am seeking to serve people rather than forcing my way on them. Jesus is relevant to today! Without Him I could not have kept up with all these demands. With Him all things are possible and I know that He will never let me down when I need Him.

Objection 2–Christian Ethics Are Not Applicable to the Business World.

Another popular objection rests on the assumption that the business world in general, and the manager's world in particular, have their own ethical systems and Christian ethics are not compatible with the realities of this competitive society. Its proponents say that if you turn the other cheek and love even your enemies (i.e., your competitors) you will always lose. They rationalize that you will not be given a fair chance so you cannot afford to give others one.

This is contrary to maintaining a living and active faith in Jesus Christ. Time and again the Scripture tells us not to worry, for if we seek to do God's will, He will provide for our every need. "Have no anxiety about anything, but in everything by prayer and supplication with thanksgiving let your requests be made known to God. And the peace of

God, which passes all understanding, will keep your hearts and your minds in Christ Jesus" (Phil. 4:6-7).

To give everything to God is to trust Him completely, knowing He will give you what you need. In management it means to commit every action, every decision to Him and to seek His wisdom in all that you do.

This is not to say that you will be a successful manager if you only believe and let God handle all the work. You cannot just sit back while angels minister to every whim and fancy. You must live the Christian life. You must work hard to apply Jesus to your work. You must learn to be a vessel that God can use in the performance of your job.

In writing to the Ephesians, Paul instructed those who were slaves on how they were to approach their labor. This teaching applies equally well to the manager.

Slaves, be obedient to those who are your earthly masters, with fear and trembling, in singleness of heart, as to Christ; not in the way of eyeservice, as men-pleasers, but as servants of Christ, doing the will of God from the heart, rendering service with a good will as to the Lord and not to men, knowing that whatever good any one does, he will receive the same again from the Lord, whether he is a slave or free. (Eph. 6:5-8)

If we carry out our managerial responsibility as though we are doing it for Jesus, we are giving it our best and we are doing God's will. The rewards will come. We need not worry about them but trust the Lord.

Objection 3—You Cannot Mix the Religious with the Secular.

Finally, there are those who complain that "religion" has no place outside of the church and that it should not be mixed with the nonreligious. If you have ever brought the Lord into a discussion about work or asked someone in the office to pray about a matter you probably noticed that you surprised even those you know to be Christians. This reaction to spiritual matters outside of what the world considers to be their proper setting is a manifestation of this objection.

This attitude often arises from an erroneous conception of the church and an equally erroneous and narrow idea of the nature of Christianity. To many, the church is the physical structure where they attend services on Sunday, and the activities which revolve around that structure. In the same way, Christianity is understood to be a religion just like Islam, Buddhism and Hinduism.

"Religion" is a word used by man to denote one sphere of his activity as distinct from other endeavors like work and play. In its true nature, Christianity is not religion, it is a way of life. To be a Christian is to be completely a Christian. The roles we fill as father, manager, employee, etc., are parts of our Christian life.

The church is not a physical structure or necessarily a group of people who come together there each week. The true church is made up of all the believers in Jesus Christ.

Those who understand this must recognize that God is present in all things and He is involved in everything we do. We can be certain that a Father who knows of the life and death of each sparrow and numbers the hairs on our heads (Matt. 10:29-31) is involved in the decision you have to make about Joe's raise or the problem you are having developing an inventory control system that meets the needs of the company.

Separation of the Spiritual
Each of these objections is part of an overall philosophy that separates the spiritual dimension of life, if admitted to exist at all, from the physical and psychological dimensions. This belief further holds that it is wrong to expect the spiritual portion of man to be the part which exercises control over man's life.

Humans are composed of body, mind and spirit. The body is man's physical nature. Our instincts, reflexes, impulses and lusts originate at this level of our existence. The sex drive, the need to satisfy hunger and thirst, and other nonthinking physical actions and reactions are dominant at this level. When man concentrates on satisfying his physical needs and lets the flesh dominate the mind and spirit, lust, gluttony and the like are the norm.

The mind is the thinking and emotional part of man. We possess intellectual ability that enables us to think, reason and make decisions. Though we wince (physical reaction) when we see the large hypodermic needle the nurse is about to use on us, we know (intellectually) that the injection will either help us heal or prevent sickness.

When the mind is in control the results are agnosticism, atheism, or an "I don't care" brand of theism, and the objections we have already discussed. Satan uses the intellect of man to let man convince himself that whatever he believes or does not believe about God is correct, and it is correct because the belief was generated by his own thought process. We are kept from the Truth because we are deceived into thinking we know the truth. Without the influence of the Spirit on the intellect, man cannot reach toward God and accept the faith He gives. Eventually we become satisfied with holding an erroneous belief and the spirit within us becomes even more repressed.

"God is spirit" (John 4:24) and our spirit is that part of us which is like God. The author of Genesis writes, "Then the Lord God formed man of dust from the ground, and breathed into his nostrils the breath of life; and man became a living being" (Gen. 2:7). The breath of life is the spirit which God has given to us to make us like Him. We cannot have life without the spirit.

Because we are imperfect and sinful creatures our spirits cannot properly direct our lives until we are under the influence of God's Holy Spirit. Once we accept Jesus as our Savior and Lord, He enters us through the Holy Spirit who pervades and takes hold of our spiritual nature. "But you are not in the flesh, you are in the Spirit, if the Spirit of God really dwells in you" (Rom. 8:9).

When we let the Holy Spirit take control, we are then able to allow Jesus to work in us and through us in everything we do. Until this occurs we continue to believe the objections and continue to put God in a remote corner of our lives rather than in the forefront where He belongs.

2

Management Today

At that time I said to you, "I am not able alone to bear
you; the Lord your God has multiplied you, and
behold, you are this day as the stars of heaven for
multitude. May the Lord, the God of your fathers,
make you a thousand times as many as you are, and
bless you, as he has promised you! How can I bear
alone the weight and burden of you and your strife?
Choose wise, understanding, and experienced men,
according to your tribes, and I will appoint them as
your heads." And you answered me, "The thing that
you have spoken is good for us to do." So I took the
heads of your tribes, wise and experienced men, and
set them as heads over you, commanders of
thousands, commanders of hundreds, commanders of
fifties, commanders of tens, and officers, throughout
your tribes. (Deut. 1:9-15)

The modern world is a mixture of organizations.
Governments, hospitals, schools, banks, churches and
businesses are all institutions that are run by managers.
Managers and organizations are like the horse and

carriage of the familiar old song; where you find one you will be sure to find the other.

From Genesis to Organization World

When God created the world and all its creatures He established the first organization and appointed Adam as its manager. "Then God said, 'Let us make man in our image, after our likeness; and let them have dominion over the fish of the sea, and over the birds of the air, and over the cattle, and over all the earth, and over every creeping thing that creeps upon the earth" (Gen. 1:26).

After man sinned and was separated from God he had to learn to take care of himself, and to do this he had to organize. Then, as now, without organization and management of that organization it would not be possible to carry out the many tasks necessary to the maintenance of life.

First, families were formed with each member being assigned certain responsibilities such as hunting, making clothing and picking berries. As the families grew into tribes the needs of the group became more complex and the extent of organization increased to include, for example, defense and the care of domesticated animals. Later, tribes joined together and continued to grow, forming nations that required an increasingly complex system of management including organization for trade with other nations.

Each level of organization developed to better achieve the basic needs of survival. As they became larger and more complex, the tasks of the manager became more difficult. The quote from Deuteronomy at the beginning of this chapter is an example of a management problem that is met by the delegation of responsibility in response to a growing complexity of organizational structure. When the Israelites came out of the bondage of Egypt they were led by one man. Before long Moses recognized it was not possible for him to personally make every decision and to give every direction, so he appointed assistants to manage at different levels.

The apostles were also confronted with the need for organization and management as the young church increased in number. Luke reports in the sixth chapter of Acts how certain men were appointed to handle the administrative duties of the community so the apostles could spend their time proclaiming the good news.

As more threads have been woven in the fabric of society the need for organization has developed to the point where: "Organization is increasingly the basic integrating principle of our society. In order to live in society we have to live organizationally."[1]

We can escape the organization world only if we are willing to live alone in a cave or on a deserted island. Most of us are employed by an organization. We all look to organizations to provide the basic services and products we need to live. It would be impossible for society to function without its institutions.

Organizations are not creatures in themselves, operating and producing automatically. They are composed of people who must be guided and directed. An organization cannot function without management any more than a man can live without a heart. Noted management scholar and writer Peter Drucker has observed, "Management is the specific organ of the modern institution. It is the organ on the performance of which the performance and the survival of the institutions depend."[2]

[1]Harvey Cox, *The Secular City* (Macmillan and Co.: New York, 1965), pp. 178-179, paperback edition.
[2]Peter F. Drucker, *Management: Tasks, Responsibilities, Practices* (Harper and Row, Publishers: New York, 1974), p. 6.

This statement is pregnant with implications about the critical role management and managers play in our society. If the society is dependent upon its institutions, and the organization is dependent on its managers, the manager becomes a most important element in society's struggle to survive.

The implications of the manager's importance are intensified when we consider that his role also carries a spiritual responsibility with it. He must work with and relate to others—his staff, employers, customers, the public, etc.; and he influences the lives of those he touches. The manager is not only a key actor in modern society, but his life and actions also have an impact on the spiritual life of many others.

Management Is . . .

What is management? First, managers are found in diverse situations. The practice of management is common to households, small businesses, government and large corporations with yearly sales in the billions of dollars. With such diversity the rule rather than the exception, no one definition will be acceptable to all. Despite this difficulty we need to consider some definitions to help us understand management. We will not attempt to develop the one best definition, but will concentrate on the key ingredients that any definition must contain.

A simple and often quoted definition is perhaps one of the best: "Management is getting things done through other people." F. Burke Sheeran has expanded on this basic definition and writes that "Management is a professional discipline that assembles and uses resources to accomplish objectives through the exercise of universal functions."[3]

If you prefer more of a systems approach, this may be helpful: "Managers are needed to convert the disorganized resources of men, machines, material, money, time and space into a useful and effective enterprise. Essentially, management is the process where these unrelated resources are integrated into a total *system for objective accomplishment.*"[4]

Many varied definitions could be added to this list but they would not add to the essential nature of the practice of management that is expressed a little differently in each of these. The first common element is that management seeks to achieve objectives, to accomplish something, to get things done. Second, the manager must get these things done through the skillful use of resources. The skills, techniques, tools and other resources needed to accomplish a specific task may vary, but all managers must work with the common resource of human beings. Money, time, space, etc., are resources also, but people are the most important and the most difficult to use.

Management is the profession of attaining established objectives through the skillful use of people and other resources. This definition emphasizes the role of people since human beings are the most necessary resource a manager has, and because without them the others cannot be used. Men are needed to operate machines, design products and to decide on the best use of available funds. People are needed to operate even the most automated factories. Objectives are not achieved without people whether they are accountants, systems analysts, salesmen or lathe operators.

Unlike other resources, people have needs and feelings

[3]F. Burke Sheeran, *Management Essentials for Public Works Administrators* (American Public Works Association: Chicago, 1973), pp. 10-11.
[4]Fremont E. Kast and James E. Rosenzweig, *Organization and Management: A Systems Approach* (McGraw-Hill Book Co.: New York, 1970), p. 7.

and they can think independently. This is why they are the most difficult resource to manage. You cannot simply flip a switch to tighten a screw to make them function properly. People have to be treated as persons and their needs must be met.

To do this the manager must be skilled in relating to others. While most people can arrange to avoid contact with those they cannot get along with, the manager does not have this option. He must work with all those who contribute to the achievement of the objective set for his work group. In management, relationships are central.

To a large degree management is a profession of human relations. The problems of people relating to one another began at the time of Cain and Abel and have not been reduced since. Jesus taught us to "love one another." He wants us all to be skilled in human relations and through His grace and love this is possible. The applicability of the teachings of Christianity to management becomes even more apparent when considering the human relations aspect of the job.

Man has always tended to ignore the divine command to seek God first and has developed his own approaches to the problems of management. In the next chapter we will look at some secular solutions to the human relations challenge and at reasons why these methods can never be completely successful.

3
Secular Approaches to Management

Let no one deceive himself. If anyone among you thinks that he is wise in this age, let him become a fool that he may become wise. For the wisdom of this world is folly with God. (1 Cor. 3:18-19)

Billy Graham has written, "We say we are a Christian nation, but much of our literature, our social practices, our deep interests, are not Christian at all. They are totally secular."[1] Approaches to management can be included in the spirit of this observation. Man has generally relied on his own wisdom, his own understanding and his own knowledge as the source of the philosophy that forms the basis for the many different approaches to management that have been promulgated, studied and adopted over the years.

In this chapter we will briefly consider some of these theories and examine how they are lacking when applied without first grounding them in the foundation of Jesus Christ. The purpose of this is not to condemn the ideas and practices to be discussed or to judge their proponents. Rather, it is proper to acknowledge that many advances

[1]Billy Graham, *World Aflame* (Doubleday & Co. Inc.: Garden City, N.Y., 1965), pp. 36-37.

in the management profession have resulted from the implementation of techniques like those discussed here. The manager should study this vast body of knowledge and apply this learning. However, on their own, these humanly designed systems are incomplete. Approached with Christ as the foundation and with the Word of God as the measure of truth, much can be found and used with beneficial results.

Classic Management Theory

Classic management theory is task focused. According to this approach it is the manager's job to find the one best way of accomplishing a given task and to control the behavior of the worker so that this pattern can be used to insure a predetermined pace of production. The focus is on the task and tends to limit the perceived needs of man to the economic realm, assuming that production will increase for better pay. This undermines the integrity of the person and limits his and his employer's conception of his worth. In effect, it considers the worker, the human factor in production, to be no more than an extension of the machine.

This theory generally underlies the management of assembly line workers, though it is not limited in its application to routine and mechanical jobs. It has often been applied to accountants who are viewed as an extension of an adding machine; to draftsmen considered only necessary to move the pen; and to typists whom the manager does not recognize when the familiar typewriter is not attached. One government employee describes his perception of his supervisor's management philosophy thus: "They want us to have the speed of computers and the stamina of bionic men. They don't relate to people and their needs." When the manager accepts and works on the premises of classic theory, this is an accurate evaluation. But men are far more than machines. The Bible says:

> What is man that thou art mindful of him, and the son of man that thou dost care for him? Yet thou hast made him little less than God, and dost crown him with glory and honor. Thou hast given him dominion over the works of thy hands; thou hast put all things under his feet. (Ps. 8:4-6)

Classical approaches to management do not recognize the God-ordained stature of man. The theory contends that man's primary needs are material. This is a simplified conception of human capabilities and needs which leave all personal concern and love for the individual outside the realm of the manager, who is only to perform the task of determining the best way of using someone in the operation. Man becomes a servant to the process rather than the mover behind production.

The Dictatorship of the Manager

Anthony Jay has advanced the thesis that "The new science of management is in fact only a continuation of the old art of government. . . ."[2] In his comparison of management to the government of nations, Jay is true to the Machiavellian theory of political power, leading him to conclude:

> The only helpful way to examine organizations and their management is as something neither moral nor immoral, but simply a phenomenon; not to look for proof that industry is honorable or dishonorable, but

[2] Anthony Jay, *Management and Machiavelli: An Inquiry Into The Politics Of Corporate Life* (Holt, Rinehart and Winston: New York, 1967), p. 3.

only for patterns of success and failure, growth and decay, strife and harmony, and for the forces which produce them."[3]

While few managers would consciously agree that their organization should be directed according to the criteria Jay uses, probably a large group actually carry out their responsibilities as though they were ruling a sixteenth-century Italian city-state. These managers hold the view that an organization is a thing and is completely impersonal. They see the company or agency as independent of the people whom it employs. It is therefore independent of the moral criteria applied to individuals. Furthermore, this leads to an approach that is more concerned with the "forces" that cause something to happen than with the people who are actually involved in carrying out the tasks and are responsible for creating the "forces."

It is this kind of attitude which spawned the Watergate conspirators who felt shielded from individual responsibility by the office of the president. This thinking divorces individual accountability from corporate liability and is much more concerned with end results or products than the people who produce them.

The argument that corporate morality is distinct from that of the individual who causes the organization to act is based on the false assumption that the individual is not responsible for corporate actions. Jesus said, "For the Son of man is to come with his angels in the glory of his Father, and then he will repay every man for what he has done" (Matt. 16:27). Furthermore, we are warned: "Do not be deceived; God is not mocked, for whatever a man sows, that he will also reap" (Gal. 6:7).

[3]Ibid. p. 27.

The man cannot be judged apart from his actions. No organization structure, no tax law, no claim of corporate immunity can release a man from being answerable for his official actions and decisions. Just as the janitor is liable when he carelessly breaks a lamp with the handle of his broom, the company president is also responsible for the harm caused to the consumer by a product he knew to be unsafe. The blame cannot be placed on the organization in either case. In sum, biblical moral principles are applicable in business as well as away from the job.

Human Relations

As the shortcomings of classical management theory became more evident the trend was to shift the focus from the work to the worker. This neo-classical theory ". . . takes the position that the main task of management is to harmonize the goals of the business organization with those of the individual."[4]

The core of neo-classicism was the human relations movement which stressed that management should develop a feeling of belonging among the workers. Since management is getting things done through others, the human relations manager applies psychological principles to the employee to stimulate him to produce more. If the manager is considerate, the reasoning goes, then production and efficiency will increase.

In human relations the manager is concerned with people and the psychological principles that help him in understanding their behavior in order to manipulate the worker for the good of the organization.

The body of man's knowledge and understanding of psychological forces is growing and is increasingly consulted for solutions to a variety of problems including

[4]Thomas A. Petit, *Fundamentals of Management Coordination: Supervisors, Middle Managers, and Executives* (John Wiley & Sons, Inc.: New York, 1975), p. 95.

employee motivation, interpersonal relations, learning, coping with aging and death, crime and race relations. Despite the application of psychology and sociology to almost every area of human endeavor and every conceivable human relationship, we have witnessed little success of note. Crime increases at an alarming pace, riots break out when black children are bused to white schools, young people drop out of school, the aged are ignored by a youth-oriented society, and divorce rates soar.

If behavioral science has failed in so many areas can we expect it to succeed in management? In general, it has failed because it has been applied without the love that makes concern real. Any expressed concern is simply used as a tool to manipulate the individual and change his or her behavior for the benefit of the society and/or the organization.

Love is not aimed at changing behavior. It is not directed toward the selfish ends of the lover. Love is a giving of oneself to the other in a way that expresses genuine concern and desire to help. Jesus said, "A new commandment I give to you, that you love one another" (John 13:34).

Jesus is the model for true love. He gave himself up for all of us. His death was the ultimate act of self-giving love, the kind of love He calls us to practice. Without Jesus our love is imperfect and always made impure by selfish desires. Through Jesus our imperfect and impure human love can become pure and whole. Psychology can be a valuable tool for the manager but only when its use has been motivated by genuine love and concern for the employees.

Open Management

Similar to the Human Relations Movement but building

on more than thirty years additional experience and accumulation of behavioral knowledge, is the Open Management approach developed by Vincent W. Kafka and John H. Schaefer.[5]

Open management suggests that the manager: "1. See a situation from the other person's point of view. 2. Identify and build on an individual's strengths, rather than concentrating on how to improve weaknesses. 3. Understand and satisfy the individual's human needs."[6]

The basic human needs which the manager is exhorted to satisfy are listed by the authors as: economic security, the need to be controlled, recognition, feelings of personal self-worth, and the need to belong.[7] These are all valid human needs but the spiritual needs of the person are not considered. Herein lies the weakness to an otherwise sound approach to managing others.

Man is primarily a spiritual being with physical, mental and social attributes. He has spiritual needs that must be met just as he has needs that correspond to the physical, social and psychological aspects of his existence. If this is so, why does open management, while placing such an emphasis on meeting the needs of the worker, fail to address the spiritual needs of the person? It ignores the spiritual man because it is a human-centered rather than a Christ-centered approach. Only in and through Jesus Christ can man be spiritually satisfied.

Paul understood the whole nature of man and the way in which spiritual needs are met. "That according to the riches of his glory he may grant you to be strengthened with might through his Spirit in the inner man, and that Christ may dwell in your hearts through faith" (Eph. 3:16-17).

[5]Vincent W. Kafka and John H. Schaefer, *Open Management* (Peter H. Wyden, Publisher: New York, 1975).
[6]Ibid. p. 15.
[7]Ibid. p. 45.

Even the wisest and most well-constructed management theory will not be fully successful unless it is built with the spiritual nature of man foremost in the design. If it is the manager's responsibility to meet the basic needs of his staff, it is also his responsibility to let Jesus be free to work among them.

The secular ways of management are deficient in the light of Christ, the wisdom of God in Christ, the love of Christ, the eyes and the mind of Christ. They are man-centered and lacking in spiritual insight, depriving the organization of the important role the Holy Spirit plays in every area of human endeavor. Secular management theories have eyes that do not see, ears that do not hear, hearts that do not feel.

Consequences

Those managers who build on the foundation of man's wisdom as expressed in secular management thought are like the foolish builders of the following parable:

"Every one then who hears these words of mine and does them will be like a wise man who built his house upon the rock; and the rain fell, and the floods came, and the winds blew and beat upon that house, but it did not fall, because it had been founded on the rock. And every one who hears these words of mine and does not do them will be like a foolish man who built his house upon the sand; and the rain fell, and the floods came, and the winds blew and beat against that house, and it fell; and great was the fall of it." (Matt. 7:24-27)

When Christ does not form the foundation on which our entire lives are based, any undertaking, whether it is in education, medicine, law or management, will not reap the benefits bestowed on those who rely first on wisdom from above rather than the wisdom of man.

When founded on man's wisdom and knowledge rather than on God's, man's work is subject to the hindering influence of Satan as well as the likelihood of human error. In management this leads to a desire to keep Christ completely out of the practice and theory of management. Christianity is not believed to be applicable to management and it is seen as irrelevant to the organization world. This results in the most serious problem faced by managers, the dual-minded and erroneous thinking that is manifest in what can be called the dual ethic epidemic.

The Dual Ethic Epidemic

A move toward morality based on a two-pronged approach to personal ethics is undermining the base on which our society was founded. As the world becomes increasingly secular, more people are employed by organizations and are beginning to accept the root philosophy of dual ethicism. This philosophy holds that the structure, mode and foundation of ethical behavior within and between organizations is different from that which governs lives outside of the corporate environment. It is the belief that two moral standards exist that are mutually exclusive. One is applicable only to the individual's personal life. The other guides the person's behavior while at work in the organization world. It is asserted that these two different standards can be compatibly held by the same individual. Just as the manager of a supermarket wears a suit to work and changes into blue jeans when he returns home, he can put on and take off the appropriate set of moral principles to correspond to the situation he finds himself in.

This philosophy is unequivocally wrong. It is impossible to continually shift from one set of moral principles to another. Before long one set influences and dominates the other. Since they are less demanding, often more rewarding materially, and we spend a larger percentage of our time involved with work, the organization ethics gradually infiltrate the Christian's home set until they are undermined and quick to be pushed aside for convenience.

This sort of double-mindedness robs the Christian in the organization world of the blessings of a peaceful and joy-filled Christian walk. The dual ethic removes the Christian's reliance on Jesus. It weakens the faith that is needed to live without anxiety in these troubled times and makes his witness to others impotent. These people soon become Christians in name only and are faced with the difficulty of struggling through life without power to live a Christ-centered life.

There is no place in our lives for a double set of moral standards. If we try to apply two standards it is not long before we are no longer living as Christians should. Like the briers in the parable of the seed, the organization ethic rises up to choke the Word of God planted in us. Until we commit every area of our being to Christ, including our work, there is danger that the moral standards of corporate society will choke our faith. If that happens we become spiritually stagnated. Often, this stagnation leads to indifference and finally complete rejection of the gospel model.

The dual ethic is based on lies, deceptions and incorrect

assumptions about organizations and measures of success. At the foundation of the organization ethic are the opinions that institutions are impersonal, people are only one part of a complex structure, and actions taken by or against an organization have no effect on the morality of individual human beings. Once we believe this it is only a small step to say that since organizations are in themselves different than people, they must have their own ethical system. This may be called the market system, business ethics or organizational standards, but it is based on the observations and rules of man rather than the teaching of God. These ethics serve, but they do not regulate the organization.

It is not surprising that organizations become impersonalized when the trend is to focus on their function and responsibility rather than on the people who carry out that function. Most of the management theories considered here are concerned first with the organization and then the people.

From the smallest one-man business to a giant corporation like General Motors, all organizations are composed of humans. People form the skeleton and they are the blood in its veins. Any action that has an effect on the structure has an impact on the people within it and is the responsibility of the one who acts. If the action is good for the organization, it is probably good for the people. If it causes harm to the institution it will cause harm to the employees.

By focusing on the acquisition of material wealth and public honors, the ground is made fertile for the establishment of the dual ethic. Success becomes an all-consuming struggle when told that we are justified in "playing by the rules of the game" rather than obeying

God in that part of life.

Nonapology for the Dual Ethic
Since the dual ethic is founded on error the adherent finds it necessary to provide excuses which rationalize his acceptance of a double-minded way of thinking.

One such excuse is that the manager is required to pursue the best interest of the organization for which he works. In doing this he cannot be bound by personal ethics which do not apply to the organization. Rather, to be a loyal employee he can only measure his actions by the organization ethic.

The Bible tells us that it is right to be obedient and submissive to those for whom we work in order that we may serve them as though we are working for Christ (Eph. 6:5). We are to do our best for the organization because it is God's will, but we know that His will never contradicts what He has revealed in the Word. Therefore, if the organization should have us act in a way that is contrary to the Word of God, we must stand firm in faith and be like Peter when he boldly told the Sanhedrin, "We must obey God rather than men" (Acts 5:29).

Another excuse is that "you can't let others get the upper hand. If they do something to you, you have to give something right back to show you won't take it or they will take advantage of you." If you are to be loyal to the organization and you are going to pursue success, you cannot be a nice guy because "nice guys really do finish last." In the world of office politics and skirmishes you must be ready to strike out at your opponent as a matter of self-defense and survival.

Recently another supervisor in my department inadvertently used a requisition for a position I was authorized to fill. He was able to interview the best applicants and, when he found that he was using the wrong requisition and did not yet have an approved position, he kept the best application and sent me the remainder.

In such a situation the organization ethic says I have the right to immediately leap to the defense of my position and demand an opportunity to interview the applicant. I would complain to the personnel department and bring it to the attention of the department head. I would seek every opportunity to avenge myself by making things as miserable as possible for my adversary. By doing this I would insure that he would not so easily cross me again.

I did not respond this way because I knew that it was not Christ's way of handling it. When Peter asked Jesus, "Lord, how often shall my brother sin against me, and I forgive him? As many as seven times?" (Matt. 18:21). Jesus told him that our forgiveness should be unlimited. "I do not say to you seven times, but seventy times seven" (Matt. 18:22). God's Word tells us to apply the principle of forgiveness out of the love we are to have for all men, even our enemies and those who would sin against us (Rom. 12:17-21).

Knowing God's will in the matter I told the other manager I understood the mistake and I asked for his recommendation concerning the applicants he had forwarded to me. In the end we both found good people for our staffs and came closer to one another in the process, building up a new level of respect and trust that previously had not existed.

Finally, there is the excuse that is bound up in the misconception of what kind of success we should be striving to attain. The organization ethic would accept just about any route that brings material success or builds the ego. This is justified by the contention that we are competing in a struggle that is bound by few rules and these rules are not compatible with Scripture because it has no place in the organization world. Those who rely on this excuse ask how they can have a fair chance if the competitors are not on equal footing. They say you have to do what the others do if you want to achieve success.

There is nothing wrong with hard and honest work to earn recognition at what you undertake provided you do it in a way approved of by God. If success is attained through sinful means it will not be lasting. But if you have reached some level of prosperity or recognition by adhering to the will of God, you can be sure that the reward is a gift from your Father who is pleased with you.

In regard to this, Jesus said: "For whoever would save his life will lose it; and whoever loses his life for my sake, he will save it. For what does it profit a man if he gains the whole world and loses or forfeits himself?" (Luke 9:24-25). If we give ourselves to Jesus we will have the success He wants us to have both in this world and eternally. If we fail to follow the Lord and seek to satisfy ourselves through worldly pursuits, our success will only be temporal and will result in spiritual poverty.

The dual ethic is the end result of the blind application of secular, nonspiritual approaches to our understanding of the organization and to the practice of management. Its strongest adherents are those who choose not to give Jesus every part of their lives. They say, "I go to church on Sunday, tithe, read the Bible some, work on the building committee and even teach a Sunday school class. I give the church money and time. Around the church and home I dedicate my life to God. Why should I give Him more?" The answer to this question is the subject of the next chapter.

4

The Answer

I am the light of the world; he who follows me will not walk in darkness, but will have the light of life. (John 8:12)

I am the way, and the truth, and the life; no one comes to the Father, but by me. (John 14:6)

The dual ethic and related philosophies which support the various secular approaches to management are grounded in darkness and deception. This deception has gone unnoticed because the great deficiency of the secular management approaches is that they lack Christ. They fail to recognize that Jesus Christ is central to all human undertaking, including the practice of management.

This is not to say that the teachings of Jesus should replace or supplant human scholarship and work. We do not mean that all management theory and techniques are to be thrown out. The scholarship, the thinking, the experimentation and hard work of those interested in management are valuable and must be used by the manager. However, unless man's knowledge is used in the light of the eternal truths God has revealed to us, it is deficient. Jesus does not teach us how to be managers but how to live as children of God. If we can learn how to live as God's people we will become better managers. Thus, the art of management, as well as every human activity, cannot reach its fullest potential unless it is grounded in Christ.

The Bible says, "Blessed are those who keep his testimonies, who seek him with their whole heart, who also do no wrong, but walk in his ways!" (Ps. 119:2-3). Furthermore, "Fear God, and keep his commandments; for this is the whole duty of man" (Eccles. 12:13), and "You shall love the Lord your God with all your heart, and with all your soul, and with all your mind" (Matt. 22:37).

These Scriptures tell us that man is to give himself wholly to God and serve Him with all his being. It is not acceptable for a man to give part of himself to the organization and the rest of himself to God. "No one can serve two masters; for either he will hate the one and love the other, or he will be devoted to the one and despise the other. You cannot serve God and mammon" (Matt. 6:24).

This is exactly what too many managers strive to do, soon finding that they are never able to adequately perform either task, serving God or serving the organization. What they need to do is to give themselves to God and to serve the organization through God. Doing this will not eliminate the temptation and the pressure to make the job the master of part of our lives, but it will place God first and by so doing we will receive the grace that we need to overcome the temptation. It also provides the illumination of Jesus Christ, by which to examine the secular ways of management so that we can glean what is good and throw away that which is based on deception and twisting of the truth. Whatever the profession or work, we must first be disciples of Christ if we are to fulfill the purpose for which we were made.

Do I Have to Give It All To God?

"Why does being a disciple mean that I have to give all of my life to God? Didn't He make me with a free will or does He want me to be a robot?"

God did make us with a free will and an intellect so that we would be able to make decisions and to exercise freedom of choice. We are always free to accept or reject Christ. We are always free to give only part of our lives to God or to give all to Him. We are free to obey or disobey our Father. If we choose to obey we must choose to give Him all of our life because that is what He demands. Unless we earnestly seek to surrender all to God we are not being obedient to Him by living the life He desires. Regardless of our profession, God wants us to live a life that is holy and dedicated to Him, and this means living in obedience.

Second, if we are seeking God's direction in one area of life, we cannot expect Him to give that direction unless we desire it for all areas of life. God wants to have a relationship with the total person. Just as a manager cannot realistically ignore domestic problems that affect an employee's performance on the job, God cannot ignore the rest of the person when dealing with one part of his life. God never forces His way into places and never violates our free will. We must choose to let Him into every compartment of our person before He will be able to minister to us.

If all the other parts are in perfect condition, but the car's battery is dead, the car will not start. Without the battery all the other parts are useless. People are similar to the car in this respect. Our lives cannot be divided into self-sufficient spheres. The job is intertwined with the family and both the job and the family are intertwined with the church. The kind of day we have had at the office or factory has an effect on how we react to the children when they are playing cowboys and Indians around the coffee table while we try to relax before dinner.

If we try to shut God out of our job we are just as effectively keeping Him out of the family, our social relationships, and every other role we find ourselves in. For years I primarily sought God in church-related activities. Occasionally I let the Lord come into my family relationships but I never sought His direction for my education, my career, or my after-work pursuits. I never experienced a closeness to God when I was doing this nor was I ever conscious of Him working in my life.

I always sought to solve my problems and difficulties by myself or with the help of other people. I was seldom at peace and I could not say that I had ever had a prayer answered. When I finally surrendered to the Lord my perspective began to change. I could see God's hand in every situation from a tender moment with my children to a potentially volatile advisory board meeting or an interview with a job applicant. As I progress in the life in the Spirit, answered prayers become ever more numerous.

The key to this transformation was that I admitted my own inadequacy and let Jesus come into all areas of my life. That does not mean that I was able to submit all of myself to the Lord at once. That is impossible because I am still learning about parts of my being I have not yet fully surrendered. What has happened is that as soon as I become conscious of a portion of me that I have not laid down, I do so. As the Lord shows me other secret places, I give them to Him. Gradually, I am dying to myself and taking on more of Christ that I may live for Him alone.

It is this kind of experience that Keith Miller describes when he writes: "Christ is tearing out the partitions in men's souls between vocation, church, and home and making a one room dwelling place for Himself in their whole lives."[1] If we want God to do this in our lives, we must be prepared to give Him everything, holding nothing back from His scrutiny, dying to ourselves, and entering His presence as an empty human being who desires only to be filled with His love.

The Answer

For every problem man faces the answer must ultimately be found in the truth, and that truth is Christ. Jesus became man, was crucified and rose from the dead to provide us with the solution to every difficulty we face. Billy Graham comments:

> I say that these [race and war] and all other problems can be solved, but only at the cross. The cross of Christ is not only the basis of our peace and hope; but it is also the means of our eternal salvation. The object of the cross is not only a full and free pardon; it is also a changed life, lived in fellowship with God.[2]

Rather than approaching management problems alone and armed only with secular theories and methods, the manager can face these same challenges with Jesus, armed with the power and authority of God, which is bestowed upon us through the Holy Spirit.

[1]Keith Miller, *The Taste of New Wine* (Word Books: Waco, Texas, 1965), p. 18.
[2]Billy Graham, *World Aflame*, p. 124.

To appropriate this we need to accept Jesus as Lord and Savior and submit to Him. "If any one serves me, he must follow me; and where I am, there shall my servant be also; if any one serves me, the Father will honor him" (John 12:26). We must be ready to respond to the invitation to follow Jesus as the original disciples did when they were called. By giving everything to God and following Jesus we are assured that we will have an unfailing and loving guide through life. Though we might step off the path and stumble, the Lord's loving hand will lift us up, heal the bruises through which we learned our lesson, and continue to provide for us.

Without God, we are helpless. "God made you and me, and He alone knows how to run your life and mine. We could make a complete wreck of our lives without Christ. When He is at the controls, all goes well. Without Him we can do nothing."[3]

When Jesus is in control the manager is capable of being fulfilled as a person and as a professional. Without Jesus, the manager must rely on his weak, human ways of doing things, lacking the wisdom and strength that can only be provided through the Holy Spirit. "Therefore, if any one is in Christ, he is a new creation; the old has passed away, behold, the new has come" (2 Cor. 5:17). When you become a new person in Christ you are fulfilled in the sense that you are capable of living for the purpose God created you: to worship, praise and serve Him in communion with Him. The manager's job and his ability to do it changes in the light of Christ. The endless paperwork and problems with staff become new opportunities for bringing glory to God. In Christ the manager can find the peace that relieves him of the anxieties that would normally rob him of his ability to perform effectively.

[3]Ibid., p. 176.

Free from the drain of anxiety and strife, the manager can turn to more creative and meaningful tasks.

I remember one of the first times I hired someone after I began to walk with Jesus. Among the many qualified and relatively equal candidates was a close brother in the Lord. In the flesh I would have spent most of the two weeks of interviewing candidates trying to find the best way to hire my friend while making the immediate supervisor of the position feel he had done the choosing. However, I knew that I must submit the hiring to the Lord and let Him place His person in the position. Even then, I was tempted to force my brother into the job though he was not the best qualified. I resisted the temptation and spent my time seriously considering the applicants until the supervisor and I were able to make a joint decision. We did not choose my friend, but someone else who clearly was better qualified for the job. I was only able to do this because I gave all the worry to God and sought His counsel in making the decision. In this instance, I claimed and acted upon Paul's advice to the Philippians:

> Have no anxiety about anything, but in everything by prayer and supplication with thanksgiving let your requests be made known to God. And the peace of God, which passes all understanding, will keep your hearts and your minds in Christ Jesus. (Phil. 4:6-7)

As an incomplete man, a man without the indwelling Holy Spirit, the manager cannot succeed in meeting all the responsibilities that are his. Only with Christ can he advance from the position of manager to pastoral minister and have the power in which to face problems, seek solutions, and meet challenges. He can stand on the promise that "My God will supply every need of yours according to his riches in glory in Christ Jesus" (Phil. 4:19).

We must return to the foundation. If man's foundation is himself or his fellow-men, his attempts to resolve the problems that face him, and to live in peace and harmony with others in every situation, will collapse in the storm of sin. Man can stand firmly against the world and be capable of dealing with the most difficult situations only when Jesus is the foundation on which he builds his life.

PART II

THE MANAGER
AS DISCIPLE

5

Knowing the
Head Shepherd

I am the good shepherd; I know my own and my own
know me, as the Father knows me and I know the
Father; and I lay down my life for the sheep. (John
10:14-15)

In the last chapter we said that the manager's life must
be founded on Christ. This chapter deals with the
relationship between Jesus and the individual and is the
beginning of a discussion of what it means to be a disciple
of Jesus Christ. It is important that we understand this,
for unless we have a sound relationship with God we
cannot have good relations with others. The first step to
being a Christian manager is understanding what it
means to be a disciple.

The Nature of Discipleship
Webster's New World Dictionary tells us that being a
disciple "implies a personal, devoted relationship to the
teacher of some doctrine or leader of some movement."
Thus, to follow Jesus, to be His disciple, means that we
become personally devoted to Him.

One contemporary authority says: ". . . what makes a person a disciple is faith in the saving mission of Jesus. . . . One is a disciple forever, for the condition of disciple is complete in itself, summed up in surrender to the Person of Jesus, who is the founder of the kingdom."[1]

In the fifteenth century, Thomas à Kempis captured the essence of discipleship in the following passage in which we can imagine Jesus speaking to us:

> It is My will, therefore, that you learn to have a perfect abandonment of yourself and a full resignation of yourself into My hands, without contradicting or complaining, and follow Me, for I am the Way, I am the Truth, and I am the Life.[2]

In these quotations and throughout the New Testament, emphasis is placed on abandonment of oneself in complete surrender to Jesus. Discipleship is more than receiving salvation, it is giving one's entire being to Christ in recognition that He is Lord. Jesus gave all of himself for us because He loves us, "Greater love has no man than this, that a man lay down his life for his friends. You are my friends if you do what I command you" (John 15:13-14). In return He asks us to give ourselves to Him: "If any man would come after me, let him deny himself and take up his cross daily and follow me. For whoever would save his life will lose it; and whoever loses his life for my sake, he will save it" (Luke 9:23-24).

Knowing Jesus

An army does not surrender until it understands the nature of the force it is confronted with. Likewise, we cannot surrender to Jesus unless we know the One to

[1]*The New World Dictionary–Concordance To The New American Bible* (Collins—World: Cleveland, 1970), p. 135, paperback.
[2]Thomas à Kempis, *The Imitation of Christ*, Harold C. Gardiner, S.J. ed. (Doubleday & Co., Inc.: Garden City, N.Y., 1955), p. 192, Image Books Edition.

46

whom we raise our hands in submission. Only by knowing and understanding one another can a close personal relationship form. It is impossible to follow Jesus unless we know Him as both God and man, rather than just as a man, as a historical figure, or only as God. It is one thing to know Jesus the man but this is not enough. Jesus must be known as the Christ, the Son of God, the Anointed One, who became man to save us from sin and give us eternal life. He can be understood as this only if we know Him in a spiritual as well as an intellectual way. When Peter confessed that he believed Jesus to be the Messiah, the Master answered: "Blessed are you, Simon Bar-Jona! For flesh and blood has not revealed this to you, but my Father who is in heaven" (Matt. 16:17).

Peter could know Jesus in the spiritual sense because God's own Spirit revealed it to him in his inner man. He lived with, ate with, spoke with and followed Jesus the man but he did not truly know Jesus until his spirit could witness that He was the Savior.

The distinction between the two ways of knowing Jesus is made clearer when we compare Peter's knowledge of the Lord with that of the people of Nazareth. These people had seen Him since He was a child but only knew Him as a man. When He preached to them they responded with their minds, not with their hearts as Peter had.

"Where did this man get this wisdom and these mighty works? Is not this the carpenter's son? Is not his mother called Mary? And are not his brothers James and Joseph and Simon and Judas? And are not all his sisters with us? Where then did this man get all this?" And they took offense at him. But Jesus said to them, "A prophet is not without honor except in his own country and in his own house." And he did not do many mighty works there, because of their unbelief. (Matt. 13:54-58)

The Nazarenes did not know Jesus as fully as Peter did and they received a different response from the Lord. He blessed Peter because of his faith and did few works for the people of Nazareth because they did not believe. We must respond as did the apostle, not as one of the Lord's neighbors but as one of His sheep.

Knowing Christ as Shepherd
The tenth chapter of John's Gospel gives some insight into the manner in which we want to know Jesus. In this chapter our Lord likens himself to a shepherd and His followers to sheep:

He who enters by the door is the shepherd of the sheep. To him the gatekeeper opens; the sheep hear his voice, and he calls his own sheep by name and leads them out. When he has brought out all his own, he goes before them, and the sheep follow him, for they know his voice. A stranger they will not follow, but they will flee from him, for they do not know the voice of strangers. (John 10:2-5)

The shepherd has a close relationship with his sheep. The sheep know they can trust their shepherd who protects and cares for them. They know their shepherd so well that they will not respond to anyone else. The relationship between the disciple and Christ must be an intensely personal one built upon the disciple's trust and faith in the Lord. When you accept Jesus as Lord and become His disciple, "The Spirit of God really dwells in you. Any one who does not have the Spirit of Christ does not belong to him" (Rom. 8:9).

The disciple is more than a follower. Being a disciple involves more than simply knowing Jesus, and more than surrendering oneself to Him. The disciple becomes like Christ through the presence of the Holy Spirit. "For those whom he foreknew he also predestined to be conformed to the image of his Son, in order that he might be the first-born among many brethren" (Rom. 8:29).

The Call to Discipleship

The call to follow is made to all men. God loves us and sent Christ Jesus because "it is not the will of my Father who is in heaven that one of these little ones should perish" (Matt. 18:14). Christ did not die on the cross for only a few but bore the sins of all. He is now calling us to answer His summons—to give our lives to Him, to be His.

Our birth into the world from our mother's womb is our first step in life. The first step in the life of discipleship is to be born again. "Truly, truly, I say to you, unless one is born anew, he cannot see the kingdom of God" (John 3:3). To be a disciple and to receive eternal life, a man must be born of the Holy Spirit to live spiritually, just as he must be born of the flesh to live a physical life.

Why is this necessary? You will begin to understand why if you take a careful and honest look at what is happening in the world around you. Crime and violence are rampant. In most of the world's cities you cannot safely walk down a street after dark. This disposition to violence is reflected in popular television shows and movies. Pornography, homosexuality, prostitution and other sexual perversions are becoming commonplace and considered by many to be normal and acceptable.

The environment is polluted. The air smells and life is dying in our waters. Smog conditions in major cities are responsible for numerous deaths because people cannot breathe the foul air. Famine and drought exist in the same world in which man has developed an advanced technology that is capable of placing men on the moon and developing a space shuttle. Despite all our knowledge and our achievements, we cannot clean up our air and waters, we cannot find a way to feed those who are starving, and we cannot enforce the law.

In simple terms, *the world is a mess!* We have not been able to overcome the poverty, strife, conflict, wars, disease and other maladies that plague mankind. Man cannot solve these problems because he is faced with something that is much greater than he, yet he is trying to deal with it through his own puny wisdom. If man is to find a solution for the mounting problems that face him, he must turn to God and seek His wisdom. "Trust in the Lord with all your heart, and do not rely on your own insight" (Prov. 3:5). Speaking through the prophet Isaiah, God tells us:

> For my thoughts are not your thoughts, neither are your ways my ways, says the Lord. For as the heavens are higher than the earth, so are my ways higher than your ways and my thoughts than your thoughts. (Isa. 55:8-9)

The world's condition is the result of sin and the evil that is caused by sin. Paul says, "I have already charged that all men . . . are under the power of sin" (Rom. 3:9) and, ". . . since all have sinned and fall short of the glory of

God" (Rom. 3:23). The condition of the world, the many confused and tormented lives of those caught in the trap of sin, the filth that pervades society—these things form a testimony to the power and pervasiveness of sin and man's inability to overcome it.

Because man is not capable of straightening himself out, God, in His wisdom and mercy, sent Jesus Christ to us. "He has delivered us from the dominion of darkness and transferred us to the kingdom of his beloved Son, in whom we have redemption, the forgiveness of sins" (Col. 1:13-14).

Our redemption and salvation was won for us by Jesus Christ, "who was put to death for our trespasses and raised for our justification" (Rom. 4:25). In His death and resurrection, Jesus defeated Satan once and for all and has provided us with a new life. To receive this new life, to appropriate the gift of salvation, we must reach out and ask Jesus to enter our lives, to be our Lord and Savior. There is no other salvation, no other way to eternal life. All of man's schemes and solutions have failed and will continue to be useless. It is only in the cross and the empty tomb of Jesus that man has hope.

The gift is yours for the asking. If your earthly father offered you a new car, you would probably accept it with little hesitation. If you would take a gift from him, why not accept a more precious gift from your heavenly Father?

Compatibility of Discipleship and Management

Once you accept Jesus as Savior you are newly created as a child of the King. However, to become a disciple you must submit to Him as Lord of your life. We often hesitate to take this second step because we are afraid that the

Lord will call us to enter a convent or become a missionary to the heathen in the jungles of Africa.

To open the way for a life of discipleship we must be freed from such thoughts because they are simply not true. Christ calls men from all professions to be His disciples. Among the first twelve Jesus called to follow Him were Matthew, a tax collector, and Peter, Andrew, James and John, all fishermen. Paul was a tentmaker and, before he came to Jesus, he was a persecutor of the early Christians. Luke is referred to as the "beloved physician" (Col. 4:14). In the book of Acts there is reference to Simon, a tanner (Acts 10), and Lydia, a dealer in purple goods, a merchant (Acts 16). These people are all from diverse backgrounds with different trades and professions yet they have one thing in common: they are all disciples of Jesus Christ. Some, like Paul, became virtually full-time ministers of the Word, and even he had to work at making tents while carrying out his mission. Others were expected to remain in the work they had been doing, serving God in their jobs.

The Lord wants everyone to be His disciples in the fullest sense. Regardless of the importance of the position he holds in the world, a manager does not have to be of the world. He can divorce himself from the world while remaining in it to carry out the tasks the Lord has assigned. A disciple can only serve the Lord in the world and a manager can only fully function as a manager in the world. The two roles are compatible. The difference is in which role becomes subordinate to the other. To be a disciple, you must follow Jesus first and be a manager only as His disciple.

We have defined discipleship, but being a disciple is much more than determining how well we fit the definition. Discipleship is a way of life and it is he only way that Jesus calls us to follow. In the next chapter we will briefly consider some of the primary characteristics of the life of discipleship.

As we leave this introduction to discipleship and before we more closely examine the kind of life we are called to pursue, let us pause to meditate on the following passage from *The Imitation of Christ*. Imagine Jesus speaking to each of us in firm but gentle tones:

> If you would come to that life, keep My commandments; if you would know the truth, believe My teaching; if you would be perfect, sell all that you have. If you would be My disciple, forsake yourself; if you would possess the blessed life, despise this present life; if you would be exalted in heaven, humble yourself here on earth; and if you would reign with Me, bear the Cross with Me, for, truly, only the servants of the Cross will find the life of blessedness and of everlasting light.[3]

[3]Ibid.

6

The Life of Discipleship

He who loves son or daughter more than me is not worthy of me and he who does not take his cross and follow me is not worthy of me; He who finds his life will lose it, and he who loses his life for my sake will find it. (Matt. 10:37-39)

To effectively minister the love of Christ to those in our charge, we must go beyond the initial commitment to our Lord and learn to live as a disciple. The first step in this life is the establishment of a personal relationship with God the Father through submission to Jesus Christ as Lord and Savior. Obedience is essential in man's relationship with God. This submission is the essential act of obedience through which the individual establishes a right relationship with God. Once this is done, relations with others can be put in order and grounded in love. This love is more than emotion and is exhibited only as we put it into action in service for our brothers and sisters.

Relationships are perfected to the degree that we learn to die to our own selfish desires. Our obedience, love and service become more Christ-like as the old self dies and we take on the character of Christ. Finally, the disciple must live a life of self-denial, obedience, love and service in a world that is hostile to him because this life is not compatible with the ways of the world.

In this chapter we will separate each of these intertwined qualities which characterize discipleship and briefly study them. However, before we begin this discussion it is important to make a special note of why this chapter finds its way into a book about management. It is here because each manager who would follow Christ must understand what it means to be a disciple, for it is only by living as a disciple that the manager can minister to the people on his staff. One cannot deal with spiritual matters unless his own spiritual house is in order, and other difficulties can be faced more confidently knowing that the Lord who made and knows all is working in you.

Placing God First

I am the Lord your God . . . you shall have no other gods before me. You shall not make for yourself a graven image . . . you shall not bow down to them or serve them. (Exod. 20:2, 3, 4, 5)

But seek first his kingdom and his righteousness, and all these things shall be yours as well. (Matt. 6:33)

There is only one true God to worship, one God to whom we are to submit. If we have placed money, work, organization, status, or anything other than God in the first place in our lives, we have made a false god and, therefore, we worship an idol. The person who sets God on the shelf to be taken down on Sundays or special occasions, but not to be taken to work, has violated this commandment. God alone is worthy of having first place in our lives. It is to Him we owe our being. Is it wrong to give ourselves to the One who has given us all? We can only make commitments to others and place value on other things in proper perspective to our wholehearted submission and devotion to the Lord.

When we give God first place in everything we do, when we seek His will in every decision, we are saying "yes" to the invitation of Jesus to "follow me." Being a disciple means giving our entire being to God. When we put all things—job, family, wealth, even our own welfare—after our relationship with our heavenly Father, we are making possible all the demands of the life of discipleship.

In a right relationship with God we desire to do nothing contrary to His will for us. We want to live according to His Word. We want nothing to come between us and God. As managers we must learn to submit all decisions and actions unto the Lord, and every personal relationship must be governed by selfless love. No business deal, no personnel decision, no change of jobs can become more important than the proper relationship with the Lord. Remember that Jesus warned, "For what will it profit a man, if he gains the whole world and forfeits his life?" (Matt. 16:26). Nothing has more value than eternal life in God's presence and we are guaranteed this life when we choose to seek Him above all other things.

Thus, the first responsibility of the Christian manager is to love and serve God. All else, the way he performs his job, the way he serves his employer, the relationship he has with his staff, everything he does must be subordinated to his relationship with God.

This may cause particular hardship for the manager in a

secular organization. He may be required to refuse to carry out assignments that would be contrary to God's will. He may have to forsake promotions or other rewards and accept the sting of ridicule from nonbelievers. He may even have to resign if he cannot do the job he is given because it would not be consistent with a life characterized by wholehearted devotion to the Lord.

This is part of the cost of discipleship, a cost the Christian manager must be aware of. He cannot be a disciple unless he accepts this cost. If he is to remain loyal to Christ in his calling as a manager he cannot allow his job to take a more prominent position in his life than God.

We cannot be transformed into the image of Christ until we can put aside all else. Just as Jesus cleansed the temple of the crooked moneychangers and their animals, we must allow the Holy Spirit to cleanse the temple of our spirits—removing all idols whether they are power, money, position, or some other self-satisfying thing. Each of these blocks our relationship with God and must be crucified with our sins if we are to be disciples.

Obedience

He who has my commandments and keeps them, he it is who loves me; and he who loves me will be loved by my Father, and I will love him and manifest myself to him. (John 14:21)

Before we can begin to live as children of the Father we must fulfill the first requirement of Christian obedience and make God first in our lives by receiving His Son as Savior and Lord. Without obedience we are not saved. The life of the disciple begins with an act of obedience and is carried out in faithful obedience.

Jesus was perfectly obedient to the Father and was therefore pleasing to Him. His perfect relationship of mutual love with His Father grew from this. He said, "For I have come down from heaven, not to do my own will, but the will of him who sent me" (John 6:38). He had no interest in pleasing himself. Everything He did, carpentry work, healing the sick, preaching the kingdom, and finally giving His life, was the will of God. He sought only to bring glory to God through His obedience. In this, we need to follow the example of our Savior.

Listening to Jesus

We can learn obedience by listening to Jesus, by hearing and responding to God's incarnate and written Word. At the wedding feast at Cana, referring to Jesus, Mary told the servants, "Do whatever he tells you" (John 2:5). The servants obeyed and were blessed with a miracle. The disciple must learn to tune his spiritual ear to the voice of the Lord and always act on this direction.

The first eleven verses of the fifth chapter of Luke's Gospel relate the call of Peter, James and John, and give an excellent example of the obedience which is part of discipleship.

> While the people pressed upon him to hear the word of God, he was standing by the lake of Gennesaret. And he saw two boats by the lake; but the fishermen had gone out of them and were washing their nets. Getting into one of the boats, which was Simon's, he asked him to put out a little from the land. And he sat down and taught the people from the boat. (Luke 5:1-3)

The fishermen worked hard through the night, for that was when fishing was likely to be successful. This scene took place in the early morning, not long after sunrise. Peter and his companions had finished their work and were in the process of cleaning up and putting away their gear. They were probably hungry and tired and in a hurry to get home for some breakfast and a chance to sleep. When Jesus asked Simon (Peter) to use his boat, the fisherman put the will of the Lord ahead of his own desires.

And when he had ceased speaking, he said to Simon, "Put out into the deep and let down your nets for a catch." And Simon answered, "Master we toiled all night and took nothing! But at your word I will let down the nets." (Luke 5:4-5)

After hearing the Lord speak, Peter was asked to do what he, the professional fisherman, knew was almost impossible on this lake, to catch fish in daylight. Despite already having completed the tedious task of washing the nets, which would have to be repeated after lowering them this time, he obeyed the Lord's word. The presence of Christ aroused enough faith in Peter for him to obey regardless of the seeming foolishness of the task.

And when they had done this, they enclosed a great shoal of fish; and as their nets were breaking, they beckoned to their partners in the other boat to come and help them. And they came and filled both the boats, so that they began to sink. (Luke 5:6-7)

The reward for obedience was such an overflow of God's

blessings that they had to be shared with others. Peter listened to the Lord, obeyed Him, acted in faith, and received his reward out of the abundance of the Father.

But when Simon Peter saw it, he fell down at Jesus' knees, saying, "Depart from me, for I am a sinful man, O Lord." For he was astonished and all that were with him, at the catch of fish which they had taken; and so also were James and John, sons of Zebedee, who were partners with Simon. And Jesus said to Simon, "Do not be afraid; henceforth you will be catching men." And when they had brought their boats to land, they left everything and followed him. (Luke 5:8-11)

Peter knew he was not worthy of being with the Lord but because he recognized his sinfulness and responded to the Word of God, he was called to be a disciple. Peter was not asked a question, "Will you follow me and become a fisher of men?" He was told, "You will be catching men." He heard this and obeyed by leaving all else behind and following Christ.

Christian managers are invited to live in this obedience which comes from loving and listening to Christ. We are called to respond to the Word of God and live in obedience to it. Thus, we can find the measure for our adherence to God's will in the Scripture. Everything we do as managers must be measured by God's Word. As William MacDonald has written, ". . . the disciple's desire should be to saturate himself in the Scriptures—to read them, study them, memorize them, meditate upon them day and night. They are his chart and compass, his guide and comfort, his lamp and light."[1]

[1] William MacDonald, *True Discipleship* (Walterick Publishers: Kansas City, Kansas, 1962), p.33.

Love

This is my commandment, that you love one another as I have loved you. Greater love has no man than this, that a man lay down his life for his friends. You are my friends if you do what I command you. (John 15:12-14)

We would not be concerned with management, with discipleship, nor with eternal life, in fact we would not exist if it were not for the one basic fact that underlies all of creation: GOD LOVES US! God's love for His children is the greatest love in existence. "For God so loved the world that he gave his only Son, that who ever believes in him should not perish but have eternal life" (John 3:16).

A disciple desires in obedience to imitate his Master by living a life of love. First, we are to love God: "You shall love the Lord your God with all your heart, and with all your soul, and with all your mind, and with all your strength" (Mark 12:30). Then, out of this love of God, we are to love others.

The command to love our brothers and sisters extends not only to those we are friendly with but also to those who are enemies and would do us harm (Matt. 5:44). To love one another is to serve one another. It is to desire good for each other. It is not possible to be a disciple unless this love, which is given first to us from God, is given back to Him through our love for one another. Love can never be perfected unless it is the same love we receive from God that we in turn give.

That we are to love one another is the great principle that guides us in the life of discipleship and underlies all relationships with others. Earlier in this chapter we considered the greatest commandment, to put God first in our lives and to love Him above all things. The focus now shifts from our relationship with God to our relationships with other people. In an important and intrinsic way, the two relationships are one and can never be separated.

What Is Love?

We are not interested in the world's conception of love on which volumes of prose and poetry have been written. What we are concerned with is the purest and greatest form of love, which God, through Christ, exhibits for us and calls us to offer to all men. Surely these few pages cannot adequately examine all the aspects of this love, for it is as large and unfathomable as God himself, "for God is love" (1 John 4:8) and we might as well take on the impossible task of defining God. However, we need a point of reference from which to begin our study and it is for this reason that the following definition is offered: *Love is a completely other-directed attitude that is made manifest through service without regard for self and desires only good for the other.*

Perhaps the most meaningful commentary on love is found in Paul's first letter to the Corinthians:

If I speak in the tongues of men and of angels, but have not love, I am a noisy gong or a clanging cymbal. And if I have prophetic powers, and understand all mysteries and all knowledge, and if I have all faith, so as to remove mountains, but have not love, I am nothing. If I give away all I have, and if I deliver my body to be burned, but have not love, I gain nothing. (1 Cor. 13:1-3)

Paul is saying nothing has value—no gift, no skill, no material thing has any worth unless the possessor has love. Unless love is in your heart the fact that you are the most brilliant personnel manager in the business will be meaningless. Intelligence, education, experience—all are without value unless they are used in love and for the purposes of love. Unless our actions are grounded in love they are worthless because value or worth comes from God and without love nothing can please our loving God.

If love gives value and meaning to life then it is the greatest attribute man can possess. However we may strive, it is impossible for man to possess this kind of love by his own power. Love is a gift from God, made available to us through the death and resurrection of Jesus. John writes, "Beloved, let us love one another: for love is of God, and he who loves is born of God and knows God" (1 John 4:7). God is the source from which we appropriate love and share it with our fellow-man.

In and through Christ a disciple is free to love in all relationships. The Christian manager will love his subordinates, his superiors, his customers, all those he deals with in his job, by serving them and desiring good for them. Jesus does not pick and choose those He loves; He gives himself to all men, whether they return His love or not.

Though it is difficult at times to love some people, we know that Christ dwells in us and loves them through us. Seek to follow His example and ask Him to use you as a vessel pouring His blessing out on others. Ask to see them with His eyes and you will learn to love them as the Lord does.

Love One Another

"Therefore be imitators of God, as beloved children. And walk in love, as Christ loved us and gave himself up for us, a fragrant offering and sacrifice to God" (Eph. 5:1-2). In all our contacts with others we are to imitate the complete self-giving love that Christ gives to us. He is God but chose to serve us because of His love for us.

Our love for one another cannot be separated from our love for God. By loving others we are loving God:

> If any one says, "I love God," and hates his brother, he is a liar; for he who does not love his brother whom he has seen, cannot love God whom he has not seen. And this commandment we have from him, that he who loves God should love his brother also. (1 John 4:20-21)

Jesus' washing of the disciples' feet at the Last Supper illustrates this relationship. After performing this humble act of love He told them, "If I then, your Lord and Teacher, have washed your feet, you also ought to wash one another's feet" (John 13:14). Shortly after this Jesus said, "Truly, truly, I say to you, he who receives any one whom I send receives me; and he who receives me receives him who sent me" (John 13:20). Then He gives them the commandment, "A new commandment I give to you, that you love one another; even as I have loved you, that you also love one another" (John 13:34).

Taken together these Scriptures illustrate the inseparable bond between our love for one another and our love for God. By loving others we are loving Jesus and our Father. We cannot have a "Jesus and me alone" relationship. A personal relationship with Christ is only possible in the context of a loving relationship with others.

Service

Whoever would be great among you must be your servant, and whoever would be first among you must be your slave; even as the Son of man came not to be served but to serve, and to give his life as a ransom for many. (Matt. 20:26-28)

Jesus is our example of one who serves others. The proud man expects others to recognize his status by meeting **his** every need while he provides service to no one but **himself**. The disciple renounces and humbles himself in order to give service to others. Service is the outward sign of our love for one another. If we love, we will desire to give of ourselves. You cannot serve unless you love and unless you serve you do not love.

Christ's Example

The natural man is most interested in satisfying his own desires and satiating his appetites. When a man makes the decision to follow Christ he is choosing to set aside self-interest. Even having made this decision man is weak and of his own accord finds it difficult to learn to serve others. The disciple has Jesus as his model and by the power of the Holy Spirit he can attain this virtue.

We are great in the eyes of the world if we become one of the best at what we do. Jesus would also have His disciples be great, but in His way. He teaches that to be considered great or accepted as a leader, the disciple must be the best at serving others. Jesus' entire mission was an example of service. He healed others even when He was exhausted and hungry; He fed those who came to hear

Him; He washed the feet of His disciples; He freely gave all this of himself. He gave the ultimate service to mankind by bearing the sins of the world and giving His life for all of us. This is the example we are called to follow.

Do nothing from selfishness or conceit, but in humility count others better than yourselves. Let each of you look not only to his own interests, but also to the interests of others. Have this mind among yourselves, which you have in Christ Jesus, who, though he was in the form of God, did not count equality with God a thing to be grasped, but emptied himself, taking the form of a servant, being born in the likeness of men. And being found in human form he humbled himself and became obedient unto death, even death on a cross. (Phil. 2:3-8)

When we offer to help other people we are serving God at the same time. Jesus said, "Whoever receives one such child in my name receives me; and whoever receives me, receives not me but him who sent me" (Mark 9:37). We must learn to give ourselves to others that we may be servants of God. We must seek to help all those who come to us in need, sharing our lives, our homes and the blessings God has given us.

It is especially important for the Christian manager to understand this characteristic of service. Too often the popular idea of management is that the staff is to serve the manager by doing what he tells them to do. The Christian conception is the opposite in that it is based on the example of Christ. Jesus is our Lord and as Lord we obey Him and serve Him. Yet Jesus first served us through His incarnation, death and resurrection. It was in serving us, His servants, that God could perfectly love us and have His love fulfilled. Thus, the true practice of management is one in which the manager seeks to serve his staff, not only his superiors and clients.

In practice this means that the manager is always trying to obtain what is good for his employees whether in the exercise of his authority or in providing assistance in handling personal matters that do not always relate directly to the job. For example, by giving work assignments and insuring that they are done properly the manager is helping the employee fulfill himself by accomplishing the task and providing him with an opportunity to be productive and earn a living.

The same is true in discipline. When the supervisor is required to discipline a staff member he must do it in a way that helps the employee do a better job, to improve.

The manager also serves the staff by helping employees understand how to do a task, by counseling them when in need, by even taking on some of their work if the burden has become too great. The entire relationship of the manager to his employees should be characterized by service.

As a disciple the manager must place his interests in second place to those of his staff. His first desire should be that, in the accomplishment of the unit's objectives, his employees are properly cared for and are having their needs met. Only in serving them and helping to fulfill their needs can he himself be completed. That is, the true interest of the manager, as manager, must be that his employees are taken care of. Thus, as he serves them, that which he desires becomes his. Truly, it is in giving to his staff that the manager receives.

The Life of Discipleship

Denying Self

If any man would come after me, let him deny himself. (Luke 9:23)

Jesus gave up His throne and His kingship, came to earth in the form of a man and died in agony on the cross. He was not required to do this; He was not forced. It was because of His love for us that He freely chose to give so completely of himself. Jesus' life and His giving of the life is the greatest example of self-denial that the world has known. He put us ahead of himself. He quashed all selfish desires, lived and died, not for himself, but for others.

As disciples we should imitate Jesus by becoming humble, removing all self-seeking from our hearts, and dying to ourselves. We must make a habit of placing the needs and desires of others ahead of our own.

Discipleship is a life of obedience, love and service. Unless one denies himself he cannot be a disciple. Obedience to God requires the complete submission of our lives to Him. Love of others requires that we serve them regardless of our own wishes.

As His disciples we are to take on the attitude of Christ by becoming humble and obedient in every respect out of love for God and for our brothers. Jesus could not carry the cross until He gave up His position. We cannot carry our little portion of the cross of Jesus unless we leave behind all things that would hinder our way. We must be prepared to leave everything and follow Him like the first disciples did. We must leave behind status, pride, selfish wants, and personal satisfaction at the expense of others. We must lay each of these stumbling blocks at the feet of Christ and in their place be filled with a spirit of desire to serve God. Jesus was fulfilled by emptying himself for

69

others. We are also completed when we are emptied of all pride and selfishness. It is in this way that we achieve true personal satisfaction.

What Is Death to Self?

The ultimate act of self-denial is to give one's life for someone else. To be able to do this a person must possess a selfless attitude about the value of his own life. To accept death in another's place we must consider the other's life as being more valuable than our own. Our children and spouses are very important to us and most of us would have little trouble to willingly die in their place. This is the same attitude we are to have toward all people and we must be willing to allow the Holy Spirit to cultivate this within us. While few may actually be called to die for someone, all are called upon to crucify the natural man, preparing to give of ourselves by taking on the attitude of Christ. We are told to:

> Put off your old nature which belongs to your former manner of life and is corrupt through deceitful lusts, and be renewed in the spirit of your minds, and put on the new nature, created after the likeness of God in true righteousness and holiness. (Eph. 4:22-24)

The natural man is happiest when he is satisfying his own needs. He seeks first to bring himself success and will protect his position ahead of others. He is controlled by his appetite for all that makes him feel good, and he places the feelings and welfare of others secondary to those. The Christian must put aside these selfish desires. He is called to die to the old self and be transformed into a Christ-like person.

The Life of Discipleship

For the Christian manager, death to self especially
entails a willingness to purge all selfish interest from the
job he is given. It means doing our best to bring glory to
God, to love and serve others regardless of what it means
from a personal standpoint. Death to self means that
promotions, raises, and the like are not the motivation of
the manager but the love of God and obedience to His
Word is.

Apart From the World
I have given them thy word; and the world has hated
them because they are not of the world, even as I am
not of the world. I do not pray that thou shouldst take
them out of the world, but that thou shouldst keep
them from the evil one. They are not of the world,
even as I am not of the world. (John 17:14-16)

In the seventeenth chapter of John's Gospel Jesus offers
a prayer to the Father for His disciples. An important
part of this prayer centers around the disciples' position of
being in the world but not belonging to the world or not
being of it. Jesus does not belong to the world and neither
do His followers. Just as He was in the world to do a work,
so are we in the world for a specific task.
What does our Lord mean when He prays this? We
know a disciple is one who follows Jesus and is
characterized by a life of obedience, service, love and
selflessness. What is the contrast between the world's
way and the life of a disciple? In the sense used here the
world is that which is corruptible. The world and those of
it are polluted by sin and are in the grasp of Satan and his
evil forces. When we say a Christian is in the world but is
not of it we mean that the disciple, like Jesus, does not

belong to the corrupt world but to the perfect and pure God who created all things to be perfect. However, also like Jesus, we live in the world, are surrounded and threatened by evil, but are to remain separated from the world's way of doing things.

> I appeal to you therefore, brethren, by the mercies of God, to present your bodies as a living sacrifice, holy and acceptable to God, which is your spiritual worship. Do not be conformed to this world but be transformed by the renewal of your mind, that you may prove what is the will of God, what is good and acceptable and perfect. (Rom. 12:1-2)

Why Are We in the World?

We have been left amid corruption and sin because we have been sent to do the work of God. "As thou didst send me into the world, so I have sent them into the world" (John 17:18). If you are a manager in a secular organization you are probably surrounded by the perversion of the world at all levels of the organization and in those the organization serves. You may come into contact with other Christians but your office or factory is certainly not a community of Christian brethren. But, as a disciple, you are in that organization because God has work for you to do there that will hasten the coming of His kingdom. In this lies the crucial role of the Christian manager. Your job is not just a routine, problem-filled and unspiritual forty or more hours a week. It is a mission Jesus has assigned to you! You cannot be a part-time disciple. Every task you do must be devoted to Christ and the building of God's kingdom.

Because we are each unique and are called to do God's

work in a hostile environment, we can expect we will have to face difficulty and persecution. Jesus warns us that the disciple's life will not be easy but the reward will be great:

"Behold, I send you out as sheep in the midst of wolves; so be wise as serpents and innocent as doves. Beware of men; for they will deliver you up to councils, and flog you in their synagogues, and you will be dragged before governors and kings for my sake, to bear testimony before them and the Gentiles. When they deliver you up, do not be anxious how you are to speak or what you are to say; for what you are to say will be given to you in that hour; for it is not you who speak, but the Spirit of your Father speaking through you. Brother will deliver up brother to death, and the father his child, and children will rise against parents and have them put to death; and you will be hated by all for my name's sake. But he who endures to the end will be saved." (Matt. 10:16-22)

We will face persecution for the sake of the gospel but God will not forsake us in the time of our need. Even as He warned of the trials to come, Jesus told us the Holy Spirit will be there to support us. The short period of time we spend in the world may be difficult and filled with many trials but the reward will be great: "Rejoice that your names are written in heaven" (Luke 10:20). "I consider that the sufferings of this present time are not worth comparing with the glory that is to be revealed to us" (Rom. 8:18).

Daniel's Example

Daniel is one of the best scriptural examples of one facing the trials of being in the world but not being conformed to it. In the first chapter of the book of Daniel we learn that Nebuchadnezzar, the king of Babylon, has defeated Israel and taken her people back to Babylon as captives. Among these captives is the godly Daniel, an Old Testament disciple. Daniel and his friends, Hananiah, Misha-el, and Azariah, are God's people who have been taken from the land of Israel (representative of God's dwelling place) and forced to live in the court of the pagan-king (the world). Though they lived in the world, Daniel and his companions refused to eat the rich food that had been sacrificed to idols, for they knew it was sinful to do so. When the steward in charge confronted them with this, God granted wisdom to Daniel who suggested they be allowed to try a ten-day diet of vegetables and water. "At the end of ten days it was seen that they were in better appearance and fatter in flesh than all the youths who ate the king's rich food. So the steward took away their rich food and the wine they were to drink, and gave them vegetables" (Dan. 1:15-16).

In another place it is related how Daniel's three friends, renamed Shadrach, Meshach, and Abednego by their captors, refused to worship the image of Nebuchadnezzar and were thrown into a fiery furnace. The fire was so intense that even those who cast the young Jews into the furnace were burned but God's people were not harmed. On seeing how God protected His servants, the king said, "Blessed be the God of Shadrach, Meshach, and Abednego, who has sent his angel and delivered his servants, who trusted in him" (Dan. 3:28).

Later, Daniel refused to obey the king's decree that all men should pray to him and prayed, as he always did, to the Lord God (Dan. 6). For his disobedience to men and his loyalty to God, Daniel was thrown into the lion's den and God delivered him from harm.

In all three cases we see God's people living in the world and refusing to be one with the world despite the cost of obedience. They were persecuted, but God always delivered them from their persecutors. As God's people, their task was to bring glory to God and to proclaim His greatness to a pagan nation by remaining loyal to their Lord in the face of temptation and trial. As disciples we are called to do the same.

Discipleship

No one can ignore the call to discipleship without grave consequences. Once the call is accepted, all that we have discussed is expected of the disciple. This is not an easy life. It is costly and requires each person to break away from the mold of the world and live a life of dedication to God in the midst of a society that is becoming increasingly secular and hostile to God's people. For this he can expect troubles now and great rewards later. No one can achieve this on his own. The Hebrews could not live according to the standards of holiness as proclaimed in the Law, and Christians cannot live life according to the standards of the greater righteousness Christ has called them to, except by the power of the Spirit of God dwelling within. But the believer does not experience this power until he submits to God and receives it from Him. In the next chapter we will see what this means.

7

The Power Source

For God did not give us a spirit of timidity but a spirit
of power and love and self-control. (2 Tim. 1:7)

Up to this point we have focused on the manager as a
disciple. In the next part we will concentrate on the
manager's ministry. Being a disciple is not easy. The
requirements grow in intensity as the disciple is led into
ministry. When considering this we can either begin to
tremble or throw up our hands in disbelief. By his own
power, natural man can never hope to fulfill what is
expected. Jesus is aware of this and He still calls us to be
His followers. When the rich young man came to see Him
he asked the Lord, "Teacher, what good deed must I do,
to have eternal life?" (Matt. 19:16). Jesus told him to keep
the commandments and the man responded that he had.
Then, drawing him on to greater righteousness, Jesus
told him, "If you would be perfect, go, sell what you
possess and give to the poor, and you will have treasure in
heaven; and come, follow me" (Matt. 19:21). The man
sorrowfully went away because he was very wealthy and
could not understand how he could lay down his life, which

is what Jesus was really demanding of him. In this context Jesus told His disciples, "Truly, I say to you, it will be hard for a rich man to enter the kingdom of heaven. Again I tell you, it is easier for a camel to go through the eye of a needle than for a rich man to enter the kingdom of God" (Matt. 19:23-24).

Here Jesus is telling us that it is impossible for the natural man, bound up as he is by the world's way of life, to have eternal life. This shocked His disciples who asked, "Who then can be saved?" (Matt. 19:25). In response, He told them, "With men this is impossible, but with God all things are possible" (Matt. 19:26). On his own power a man cannot be a disciple and follow Jesus to salvation. But, through the power of God even man's weak and sinful nature will not be an obstacle. We must look to God for the power to be disciples and for the strength we need to carry out the responsibility of ministry. We must recognize that this is not human power, rather it is divine power bestowed upon us for the purpose of building God's kingdom and bringing Him glory.

The first step in receiving this power is for the person who desires it to recognize and admit that he or she cannot go it alone, that they cannot save themselves from the world's sin. When we are able to admit this we must then turn to Jesus and ask Him to take over our lives. Only you can take this action, "Because, if you confess with your lips that Jesus is Lord and believe in your heart that God raised him from the dead, you will be saved. For man believes with his heart and so is justified, and he confesses with his lips and so is saved" (Rom. 10:9-10). When we accept Jesus as Lord and Savior salvation is assured and the Holy Spirit comes to live in us, but to receive the power we need there is another step we must make in faith.

The Power Source

Power from on High

Just before He ascended to the Father, Jesus told His disciples, "And behold, I send the promise of my Father upon you; but stay in the city, until you are clothed with power from on high" (Luke 24:49). The promise is the Holy Spirit and the power from on high is the power the Spirit brings that we need to live an active and service-filled life of discipleship. This is the power that comes when we allow the Holy Spirit, who already dwells in us, to be released and overflow from us. This is the baptism in the Holy Spirit. This is what Jesus promised when He said, "You shall receive power when the Holy Spirit has come upon you" (Acts 1:8).

When we are saved we are filled with the "living water" that is the Holy Spirit. This filling is for the purpose of personal sanctification. It is the rebirth, being born of the Spirit that Jesus speaks of. This makes us children of God, guaranteeing eternal life. A definite change takes place as we are no longer of the world but of the Father's kingdom. However, the Holy Spirit must be freed in us to give us the power to serve the Lord with effect in the world. When the believer is immersed to overflowing with the Holy Spirit and the Spirit overflows from you, when you have surrendered to God and allowed Him to work freely in and through you, the power to be an effective witness to the world is manifested in you.

From the time Jesus called Peter he left everything and followed the Lord. During the three years he spent with Christ he was taught by the greatest of teachers and matured as he witnessed the love and compassion of Jesus. He certainly knew who Jesus was when he proclaimed Him to be the Messiah (Matt. 16:16) even before the transfiguration and resurrection of the Lord. Yet, when faced with the tribulation of Christ's arrest and crucifixion he denied Him three times and ran away (Matt. 26:69-75).

After He had risen, the Lord appeared to the disciples and "He breathed on them, and said to them, 'Receive the Holy Spirit' " (John 20:22). It was then that Peter was born again and was filled with the Spirit. But he was not yet living in the power of the Spirit. Any supernatural power that worked through Peter did so as the result of his direct physical contact with the Lord. Recall when Peter walked across the water (Matt. 14:22-33). As long as he kept his eyes on Jesus he walked miraculously on the waves. When he turned to look at the storm surrounding him he sank. This was because he no longer had the contact with Christ through whom the power flowed. Without the actual physical presence of the Lord, Peter was spiritually weak.

It was because of this weakness in all the disciples that Jesus did not tell them to begin the task of evangelization at the time of Ascension. Though they had received the Holy Spirit, the power of the Spirit was not yet manifest in them. Just as they had need of the physical presence of Jesus to enable them to be His disciples while He dwelt among them as man, they needed the Holy Spirit's manifest presence to enable them to live as disciples after Christ left the earth.

Peter and the other disciples were weak and uncertain as they waited in the upper room. Then, on the day of Pentecost, "they were filled with the Holy Spirit and began to speak in other tongues, as the Spirit gave them utterance" (Acts 2:4). The speaking in other tongues manifest by the disciples on that day was a sign of the overflowing of the Holy Spirit that infused the disciples with power. Immediately after this experience Peter, an uneducated fisherman, preached his first sermon and it won three thousand souls for the kingdom (Acts 2:14-41).

This was only the beginning of Peter's ministry. Throughout the book of Acts we witness the Lord's power working in and through the apostle. In Jesus' name he imparts healing (Acts 3:1-10), and full of the Holy Spirit he continues to preach God's Word and the message of salvation to even the highest court of the Jews (Acts 4). Peter was used powerfully of God from the Day of Pentecost until, as tradition has it, he was crucified upside down at his request because he did not feel worthy of being executed in the same way as his Lord had been.

What had transformed this simple fisherman from a man who would deny his Lord under pressure to a faithful servant who died for the sake of the gospel? It was the power of the Holy Spirit that began to overflow from him on the Day of Pentecost.

The first disciples began the building of the church for which Jesus had laid the foundation. They could not have done it without the power of the Holy Spirit just as we cannot continue the building of His kingdom without this power. This is why everyone who will effectively serve God must surrender himself to the fulness that is brought by the overflowing of the Spirit.

The baptism of the Holy Spirit releases the power in the life of the believer. The disciple's life is modeled on that of Jesus and our being able to carry out the tasks of ministry is dependent upon the extent to which we are molded in His image.

The baptism of the Spirit opens the full working of the

charismatic gifts in our lives. These gifts (see 1 Cor. 12:1-11) are manifestations of the power of God and are given for the building up of the body of Christ.

The action of the Spirit is manifest in the believer in many ways. When I was baptized in the Spirit I found that God's Word became more meaningful, providing a solid base on which to stand when going out into the world. I also began to see my environment with spiritual eyes that also allowed me to discern the needs of others through all the smoke screens we humans become so adept at raising. I also found witnessing, ministry, and teaching became easier as I began to rely on the Spirit to do the talking and not worry if I could do it. Most importantly, I found the strength to live and work in a hostile world while maintaining a strong and ever-increasing faith.

The released Spirit within us prepares us to function as disciples. It is the source of the energy we need for service. It is the source of the fortitude and courage that enables us to remain in the world while not being trodden under or lured back into our old ways. This freeing of the Spirit is a gift from God and is available for the asking. He wants us to have the power so we can do His work on earth. We need only be willing to surrender ourselves and to be open for all God wants to give us.

Growing in Power

A weight lifter's strength does not come all at once. He must regularly work out and exercise his muscles. Even after winning a world championship he must continue to train if he is going to stay in competition. It is the same with the disciple. The power to serve the Lord does not all come upon us at once. Being weak humans we could not handle all God could give us so we must continue to exercise our faith so that it may grow in us. The disciple's diet must include the Word of God, fellowship with other Christians, prayer and service.

The Word of God. The disciple must make a steady diet of the Scriptures. He must read, digest and meditate on God's Word every day. We must allow God to do what He promised through Jeremiah, "I will put my law within them, and I will write it upon their hearts" (Jer. 31:33). By letting God's Word become a part of us we find wisdom, knowledge, understanding, discernment, counsel and guidance (Ps. 119). We must learn to live according to the Word and rely on it at all times. The more we dwell in the Word, the more our lives are formed by the Word, the stronger we become and the more useful we are to God.

Fellowship. God does not intend for His people to walk alone. That is why He created a church, a body of believers to strengthen one another. We cannot alone attain the perfection of Christ but in the body we find all the parts we need to minister to our particular need. "For just as the body is one and has many members, and all the members of the body, though many, are one body, so it is with Christ" (1 Cor. 12:12). It is in regular fellowship with a Christian community that we minister and receive ministry. The author of Hebrews encourages us to fellowship: "Not neglecting to meet together, as is the habit of some, but encouraging one another, and all the more as you see the Day drawing near" (Heb. 10:25). Jesus ministers to each of us through the members of the body. In fellowship we can benefit from the insight of others into the Word and do not have to rely solely on our own understanding. By sharing what the Lord has taught us we can learn far more than it is possible for each one of us to attain individually. In fellowship we can share our victories and rejoice together. We can share our hurts and bear one another's burdens. As part of a worshiping group of Christians we receive direction from God by coming under the authority He has established. In the body we are fueled to go to work in the world and we can find the guidance and counsel that will help smooth our path as we go about the Lord's work. To grow we must fellowship with our brothers and sisters in Christ, both receiving and giving freely of the gifts God has given to us.

Prayer. In prayer we have an opportunity to talk with our Lord and brother and to hear Him. It is our chance to minister to Him and to be ministered to. Through the vehicle of prayer we come into a closer personal relationship with our Savior. If a marriage is to be built on firm and lasting love the husband and wife must spend many intimate moments with one another. If our relationship with God is to be strong we must spend many intimate moments with Him in regular prayer. For prayer to effectively bring us into a close walk with Jesus, it must be regular, sincere and honest. We must pray and listen as we would commune with Christ if He were physically present in our prayer closet.

Prayer is so vital to our relationship with the Lord that if we are too busy to pray and we find we fail to turn to God with regularity, we must pause to discover what has replaced prayer in our lives. If God is the primary focus of our life, then prayer is always a top priority for our time. Keith Miller beautifully expresses the meaning of prayer:

Prayer is a direction of life, a focusing of one's most

personal and deepest attention Godward. The purpose is to love God and learn to know Him so well, that our wills, our actions, will be more and more aligned with His, until even our unconscious reactions and purposes will have the mark of His love, His life about them.[1]

Prayer is essential to our relationship with God. It is no wonder that we are instructed to "Rejoice always, pray constantly, give thanks in all circumstances; for this is the will of God in Christ Jesus for you" (1 Thess. 5:16-18) and, "I desire then that in every place the men should pray, lifting holy hands without anger or quarreling" (1 Tim. 2:8). We are to pray always and everywhere and that includes at work. Every morning I pray for the day ahead. I also pray frequently throughout the day for specific situations or I take part in praise and thanksgiving. At times this is done with staff members and often for them. When I have an opportunity I open the Bible and read a few verses. I do this and encourage my staff to do this to help us maintain our focus on God during all the trials a business day can bring. Sometimes the prayers I offer are long but usually they are only a word or two in acknowledgment of the ever-present reality of my God.

The Scriptures also tell us, "I urge that supplications, prayers, intercessions, and thanksgivings be made for all men, for kings and all who are in high positions, that we may lead a quiet and peaceable life, godly and respectful in every way" (1 Tim. 2:1-2). Therefore, I pray for my staff, my superiors, my peers. Anyone I come into contact with in my job may be the subject of prayers offered to God.

Furthermore, Paul exhorts, "Have no anxiety about

[1]Keith Miller, op. cit., p. 65-66.

anything, but in everything by prayer and supplication with thanksgiving let your requests be made known to God" (Phil. 4:6). When God says to pray for everything He means exactly that. I have prayed for and seen answers to prayer for countless situations at the office including finding lost reports, potentially explosive meetings, guidance in preparing a study or writing a letter, and hiring personnel. Phillips Brooks provides sound advice for the praying manager: "Do not pray for easy lives. Pray to be stronger men. Do not pray for tasks equal to your powers. Pray for powers equal to your tasks."[2]

What can you expect if you pray sincerely and diligently? First, expect answers just as Jesus promised us, "Whatever you ask in my name, I will do it, that the Father may be glorified in the Son; if you ask anything in my name, I will do it" (John 14:13-14). Second, by turning to God in prayer we acknowledge that He is at the center of our lives. We become humble and in this humility God is able to work His grace to transform us into the image of Jesus. In prayer we also learn that whatever the situation or problem, God can work it out. We may be His instruments but it is through Him that our work is accomplished. Finally, all this adds up to assurance that we are in God's loving hands. Through prayer we are made strong, nourished and filled with God's peace.

Service. It is in service that we are given the opportunity to flex our spiritual muscles by using the gifts God has given us. As the muscles of our body increase in strength with use so do our spiritual muscles grow stronger in service. If we fail to serve, we not only fail to be obedient to God and to carry out the responsibility of discipleship, we also will weaken spiritually. The

[2]Phillips Brooks, quoted in *Living Quotations for Christians*, ed. Sherwood Eliot Wirt and Kersten Beckstrom (Harper and Row: New York, 1974), p. 23.

disciple's life is one of service, the manager's ministry makes it even more so. Service is both a responsibility and a fundamental requirement for growth.

The four spirit-builders discussed here are intertwined with one another. Knowledge of the Word of God supports us in fellowship, leads us to prayer and guides us in service. Fellowship helps to bring new light on the Scriptures, provides us with guidance to strengthen our prayer life, and supports us in service. Prayer is supportive to our understanding of the Scriptures and it must be the foundation of our relationships in fellowship, for unless we can communicate with God we cannot hope to communicate with other men. It is also a prerequisite to service, strengthening us in the knowledge that the Lord is with us always. Finally, service puts the Word into action, is carried out in fellowship, and provides us with insight to guide us in prayer.

In the foregoing chapters we have seen the need for something more than man's wisdom and power to be infused into the life of the manager. We have identified that needed item to be Jesus as manifested in the life of discipleship. And we have learned how to obtain the strength and power to live that life while remaining in the world as a manager. Now we can turn to the ministry of management for which God has equipped us.

PART III

MANAGEMENT AS MINISTRY

8

The Call to Ministry

Tend the flock of God that is your charge, not by
constraint but willingly, not for shameful gain but
eagerly, not as domineering over those in your
charge but being examples to the flock. And when the
chief Shepherd is manifested you will obtain the
unfading crown of glory. (1 Pet. 5:2-4)

To this point we have focused on the discipleship
relationship between the individual and Christ. God has
called all men to be disciples and He calls each disciple to a
specific ministry within the body of Christ. "Now you are
the body of Christ and individually members of it. And
God has appointed in the church first apostles, second
prophets, third teachers, then workers of miracles, then
healers, helpers, administrators, speakers in various
kinds of tongues" (1 Cor. 12:27-28).
The pastoral ministry is one of the most critical and
difficult ministries God appoints His people to. In this
chapter we will discuss the many respects in which the
manager is like the pastor of a church, as we seek to
understand the job of the Christian manager as a kind of

pastoral ministry.

An Understanding of Ministry

The increasing secularization of society has narrowed our perception of ministry to that which is associated with the institutional church. To the world, only those who work full-time for a church denomination and are authorized representatives of that congregation are ministers. This same misunderstanding has crept into the churches themselves so that the average member is content to attend worship services, help at socials, sit on the building committee and maybe teach Sunday school—all considered as supports to ministry and the proper functions of the lay people of the church.

All of these things and more are as validly considered ministries as that of the pastor. Webster's dictionary defines a minister as: "A person acting for another as his agent and carrying out his orders or designs." All disciples are ministers in this sense because they are representatives of Christ on earth and as such obediently carry out the will of the Father. This does not mean that all lead worship services, or all teach, or all preach, but it does means that the disciple has been assigned a specific task and it is his responsibility to carry it out as a minister of Christ.

God often meets needs through His people and this is why there are probably as many different ministries as there are needs. Each of us has been called by God to do something for Him and He equips us for the task. "And his gifts were that some should be apostles, some prophets, some evangelists, some pastors and teachers, for the equipment the saints, for the work of ministry, for building up the body of Christ" (Eph. 4:11-12).

The Call to Ministry

It is important to note that Paul first lists some particular callings and then indicates that these people have been gifted to equip the saints for the work of ministry, for the building up of the body of Christ. The saints are the believers and the clear implication is that all believers are to be prepared for ministry that edifies the body.

The true church is not a formally structured institution. It is the body of all who profess Jesus Christ as their Savior and Lord and it is not exclusive to any one denomination. Ministry is not limited to the activities of the denomination to which you belong. Your ministry is not just something extra tacked onto your life when you become a Christian. It is your vocation, your calling in the body of Christ.

Nor is ministry limited to work within the body. Christ commissioned us to "Go therefore and make disciples of all nations, baptizing them in the name of the Father and of the Son and of the Holy Spirit, teaching them to observe all that I have commanded you" (Matt. 28:19-20). This refers to the ministry of evangelization which builds up the church. While this is not the primary ministry of the manager in his management role, evangelization is a part of every outreach to those in the secular world.

To be a manager is more than simply holding a job or practicing a profession. The manager is called to care for the needs of his staff with all the love of Christ that is within him. The way he performs his job will have an effect on the growth of Christ's people whether he is working with Christians or nonbelievers. The manager serves those he works for and those who work for him. As he directs his staff in the tasks assigned he is always seeking to draw others to Christ or to a closer relationship with Him, through example, actual evangelization, exhortation and teaching. All of these things enable the manager to care for the whole person.

Even at the office the disciple must work to build the kingdom of God. This does not mean he ignores objectives of the organization and establishes a church. His first priority in the job is to accomplish what is expected of him. He will find he is better able to execute these assignments if he approaches his work by integrating management with ministry. Management cannot be separated from the realm of the spirit because man is a spiritual being. By infusing management techniques with the love of Christ, an effective ministry is established in harmony with the attainment of professional objectives. To be most effective as a manager one must also be a minister. The two aspects of the job must complement and support one another.

Pastoral Ministry

In a pastoral ministry the minister is responsible for the care of others who are under his authority. In many respects the manager is also a pastor because he has been charged with the care of his staff. To better understand the manager's calling we need to look at the nature of pastoring and the way it is similar to management.

In the Bible, God's people are often referred to as sheep and Jesus calls himself the Good Shepherd. "Shepherd" has traditionally been another term for pastor. We can learn much of the nature of this type of ministry from considering the actual responsibilities of a shepherd of real sheep and applying the lessons learned to the pastoral ministry of management.

Sheep are meek animals that need someone to care for

and tend to them. As shepherds take care of the sheep, the sheep learn to trust and rely on the shepherd in every situation. The first words of the twenty-third psalm reflect this: "The Lord is my shepherd, I shall not want" (Ps. 23:1). The Psalmist knows it is the Lord who meets all of his needs. When the shepherd is diligent and loving in his duties the sheep want for nothing and they are at peace in his care.

No one is completely self-sufficient or can truthfully deny that they live because God created them and loves them. If we honestly evaluate our lives we will all find areas in which we depend upon others, just as others look to us for many things. The manager and staff are interdependent. A shepherd is not a shepherd without sheep to provide his livelihood, and the manager must have a staff if he is to accomplish the objectives he has been given. Like the sheep, the staff requires direction, guidance and love. A manager is placed in authority over a staff because there is a need for someone to coordinate individual work assignments, make decisions, reconcile disputes, and the like. Without a manager, be he titled a supervisor, foreman, or president, the employees would work without direction and there would be no one to insure proper coordination to maximize production and reduce waste.

For example, consider a clerical pool of five secretaries. Unless the senior secretary or office manager makes work assignments there is likely to be an imbalance in the work load, causing some of the typists to have too much to do while others have the time to work crossword puzzles. Thus, like the sheep need a shepherd on whom they can depend to care for them, a staff needs a manager.

The shepherd is a leader who guides the flock. He cares

for the sheep and wants no harm to come to them so he leads them to food and drink along the safest routes. The sheep know they cannot make the journey on their own so they learn to follow him without question, without hesitation, trusting that he knows the best path for them, the path that will lead to plentiful food and security.

The manager is also a leader and guide. If his staff are to respond to his direction they must trust him. To earn this trust his leadership must be founded upon love and shown in his attitude toward them. The manager who seeks his own gain is not a leader but a dictator. This ministry requires that the manager be concerned about his staff because they are people who have complex emotional, physical and spiritual needs. In making work assignments, in establishing policies and directing operations, the manager who keeps these needs in mind will find his staff eager to follow him.

The shepherd leads the flock to grassy meadows and clear streams to provide the food and drink necessary to life. Without this provision the sheep would soon use up the available food and water in one place and would die.

The manager is also a provider. It is a critical part of his ministry to work to provide for the needs of his staff. It is his task to insure that fair wages and benefits are being paid and made available to his employees. It is he who gives encouragement through kind words and recognition of jobs well done. By actively caring for his people the manager helps to fill their need for love and by using them to their fullest ability he provides them with an opportunity to be fulfilled, to accomplish, to achieve through the work they are doing. In the spiritual realm, the manager leads his staff to the "living water" and "bread of life" that is Christ. Whatever the need, the manager should be able to provide at least part of the resources needed to address it.

The shepherd is the protector of the flock. He keeps them from harm by wild beasts, and shields them from any evil that lurks ready to pounce on the defenseless and weak. Like David, the shepherd is prepared to face bears and lions that threaten his flock. Like Christ, he is prepared to lay down his life for his sheep.

The manager wants only good for his staff. He wants them to receive the best they can from all sources. This is why the ministry of management cannot be separated from the realization of assigned objectives. By competently directing his staff in their work the manager protects them from the harm that can come if they are not doing their job. If employees do not produce what is expected they may be disciplined, lose pay or even lose jobs. If the manager truly cares for his staff he will do all he can to prevent this from happening by leading and helping each person to do his own job. When an employee is not performing up to standard, the manager should care enough to try to help the individual do better and to learn to accomplish what is expected.

The manager's protective role also extends to spiritual matters. This can include prayer, counseling and gently leading others out of darkness. For example, a secretary may be in bondage to the occult through her involvement with astrology. In such a case the manager should try to show her why this is wrong and lead her to the light of Christ. Like the gentle Holy Spirit, the manager should never try to force anyone to change but has the responsibility to point out error and present the truth to the person. This is an important part of the protective nature of this ministry.

When the sheep are injured or frightened the shepherd tends to their hurts and comforts them. The manager also brings peace to his staff through counsel and reassurance. When an employee has a problem the manager makes himself available to listen, to pray, to offer counsel, to do whatever is necessary to bring the peace of Christ to the person. He must understand that if an employee is not at peace on or away from the job, he will not be able to properly do the work. It is essential that the manager learn to recognize the signs of problems in employees and then reach out to that need to bring comfort and the soothing, tender love of Jesus Christ.

When sheep go astray it is the shepherd's job to seek them out and return them to the flock. When the young lamb begins to wander the shepherd will break its legs and carry it from place to place until the legs mend. This discipline teaches the lamb to stay near the shepherd and not stray into danger. It is our job as managers to exercise authority and discipline employees in order to keep them in line with the rest of the staff. Through the proper use of authority the manager guides the staff and helps to keep them from falling into the darkness of sin.

The shepherd is all these things to the sheep. He is the strength on which the flock relies in times of trouble and the one they look to for guidance. Jesus is all these things to us, His sheep. Jesus is the Good Shepherd and He has assigned others to care for His people for Him. The pastoral minister is called to be like God who "will feed his flock like a shepherd, he will gather the lambs in his arms, he will carry them in his bosom, and gently lead those that are with young" (Isa. 40:11).

In this the manager has an awesome and critical responsibility. He is not only answerable for his own life, but must also care for the welfare of those placed under him to the extent that he has been given authority over them. That is, he has been placed in authority over his employees in the work situation and has the responsibility to minister in this capacity. Furthermore, while he has no direct authority over what the person does away from the job, these activities come under his authority and responsibility when they affect the employee's ability to do the job (like drunkenness) or when carried into the work place (like a licentious relationship between staff members). In any case, the manager is to some degree responsible for the physical, psychological and spiritual well-being of his staff. When approached as a ministry, management becomes a profession in which the primary task is being a servant to the staff.

A manager is called to a task that requires a substantial giving of self for the sake of others. He cannot take the luxury of considering his own needs to be more important than those of his flock. If it is Friday afternoon and he is eagerly trying to finish a report so he will not have to work on the weekend and a staff member comes to him with a problem, he can only fulfill his charge by helping the employee before completing the report, even if it means foregoing a golf game or postponing a fishing trip.

Love must motivate the manager's willingness to give of himself. If we expect some sort of self-gain our motives are impure. So long as we place ourselves first we cannot have the love and compassion needed to comfort, counsel or guide someone else properly. The manager serves and cares for his flock because he loves them.

The Call

The call to a pastoral ministry comes from God alone.

No man can decide on his own to be a shepherd and then legitimately place himself in that position. He might be able to take the place and hold it by force or by false pretense, but he will never have the ministry. In the Bible we see that the apostles, the prophets, the kings of Israel and pagan nations were all appointed to the position of authority by God. Whatever position a man may hold, he will not be comfortable and successful in that endeavor unless he has been placed there according to the will of God. The Lord may allow someone to usurp a position that He has not appointed him to, but he will soon find peaceful assurance to be lacking. What the Psalmist writes is true, "For not from the east or from the west and not from the wilderness comes lifting up; but it is God who executes judgment, putting down one and lifting up another" (Ps. 75:6-7).

We are summoned to live as disciples in every part of our lives. Unlike this, we may be called to a pastoral ministry in one place and not in another. For example, at work a man might be one of many clerks who make up the mass of the office staff. At church he may be a deacon or he may be a prayer group leader with much responsibility. Another man might be a corporate president, managing thousands of employees, while at church he might be an usher or be content to arrange chairs or pass out song books at the prayer meeting.

The Lord has called me to pastoral ministry in both my work and in the prayer group to which I belong. In both cases the summons clearly came from the Lord, though at different times and in different ways. As a public administrator I took my first professional position before I knew Jesus as my Lord and I became a manager less than three months after leaving graduate school. While I was still searching for God I became frustrated with the politics and management problems I faced, so I took another administrative position with limited management functions. As the light of Christ began to fill my life I gained a new awareness of the spiritual nature of my relationships with people. I began to learn to be at peace without being in charge. I was preparing to let my boss know I was satisfied to serve in whatever capacity he needed me when the Lord unexpectedly moved me into another management position with full supervisory authority. It was in this place I began to see management as a ministry, and began to be concerned for my employees' spiritual needs.

I assumed a leadership role in the prayer group in a different manner. Before I was ready for the task I had to learn some practical lessons on the service-oriented nature of leadership and how it is God who appoints us to ministry. My own attempts at leadership floundered and I learned to be content following God's appointed. Gradually, I began to see where I could serve in the group and from there I was led into leadership.

In both instances the call came in the Lord's time and not according to my own plan. Each time it came when I was becoming comfortable in a less authoritative role and I was learning to submit to the Lord and those He placed over me. When the call came to move up, it came in ways that made it impossible to doubt the Spirit's leading.

Almost immediately, in both places, I became aware of the critical role I had been placed in. People came to me with problems, seeking guidance, and desiring the peace that was eluding them. I began to feel the weight of this responsibility and began to rely less on myself and more on Jesus as I learned how helpless I was to aid those who came to me. I came to understand and continue to learn anew that it is only Jesus who can do the necessary ministering. In both positions I am still being trained to handle the delicate and important responsibility I have been assigned.

Perhaps the most difficult lesson I had to learn was that my career as a manager is as much a ministry and calling from the Lord as the ministry I have been summoned to in the prayer community. Christians often feel the best way to serve Christ is full-time in the church or some Christian organization. If that is where He has placed you, it is the best way. Otherwise, the best way to serve the Lord is in the job you hold. The early Corinthian church seemed to have difficulty understanding this, causing Paul to write something that is very much applicable to us today: "Every one should remain in the state in which he was called. So, brethren, in whatever state each was called, there let him remain with God" (1 Cor. 7:20, 24).

If you are a manager and at peace with your professional calling remain content to serve the Lord where you are unless He clearly leads you elsewhere. God has established His people in the world and He needs us to serve in secular jobs. He wants us in those places where we can reach out and bring Christ to those who would never be touched by any conventional Christian outreach. Those of us who work in the secular world are like the servants who were sent out to invite everyone they came upon to the wedding feast of the King's son (Matt. 22:1-14). Our task is to bring those we work with closer to Christ. We do this by taking seriously Jesus' commission:

You are the salt of the earth; but if salt has lost its taste, how shall its saltness be restored? It is no longer good for anything except to be thrown out and trodden under foot by men.

You are the light of the world. A city set on a hill cannot be hid. Nor do men light a lamp and put it under a bushel, but on a stand, and it gives light to all in the house. Let your light so shine before men, that they may see your good works and give glory to your Father who is in heaven. (Matt. 5:13-16)

This is the Christian's ministry. We are salt because we are sprinkled throughout secular society and organizations bringing to them a taste of the kingdom of God. We are salt by bringing Christ to the world to preserve those who we come in contact with from the destruction of sin. We are light by bringing the goodness and love of Christ into the darkness of the world. Through the light that shines in us we reveal Jesus Christ to the world.

This is our mission. If every dedicated disciple left his or her secular job this mission could not be accomplished. The manager is in a position of authority which naturally makes him a focal point for the staff, clients, and employees dealing with his part of the organization. As such, the Christian manager has immeasurable opportunity to be a witness for Christ as he carries out his ministry in the secular world.

The Source of Authority

We have referred to the manager's authority several times in this chapter. Each time it has been identified as a key ingredient of the manager's ministry. For the manager to perform capably he must depend on the authority that is given him over the people and resources he directs and uses. Therefore, an understanding of the nature of that authority is necessary to a clear conception of managerial responsibility.

First, we must understand that "there is no authority except from God, and those that exist have been instituted by God" (Rom. 13:1). Since God is the giver of authority, we are called in obedience to exercise it as He wishes. If we use it according to our own human will, we have placed our judgment, our reasoning, before God.

Scripture provides us with many examples of God's use of authority which can be characterized as *wise, just, sparing*, and *loving*. All managers would do well to reflect on how God uses authority.

All true wisdom comes from God and wisdom characterizes all of His actions. The classic scriptural example of God's wisdom being administered through man is that of Solomon's judgment concerning the harlot's child (1 Kings 3). Solomon heard all sides of the story and determined the best way to establish the truth. He did not act rashly or according to his own whims. Many bad management decisions and much pain could be spared if managers carefully considered the whole of a situation and divorced their personal preferences before acting. When the manager acts rashly and uses his authority to satisfy his own desires he is misusing a power entrusted to him.

The wise use of authority is also the just use. In the case of Solomon he remained impartial and did not side with either of the two women. His desire was to make a just decision. Likewise, the manager cannot afford to grant favors to only certain employees. His authority must be applied equally, whether in the distribution of rewards or the execution of discipline. God considers all equal and we cannot legitimately prefer some more than others, "For in Christ Jesus you are all sons of God.... There is neither Jew nor Greek, there is neither slave nor free, there is neither male nor female; for you are all one in Christ Jesus" (Gal. 3:26-28).

The explicit exercise of authority by God is sparingly manifest. Throughout history He has allowed man to go his own way, providing guidance and warning, and only implicitly exercising His authority until man made such a mess of things it was absolutely necessary to directly intervene. The residents of Sodom and Gomorrah knew God's law but chose to disobey it. It was only after they had become so perverted and spiritually blind that they would abuse an angel of the Lord that God extended judgment on the cities.

The possession of authority is not the cause for its use. When a manager too frequently overrides the decisions of his subordinates he has either not done his job in training the people who work for him or he is seeking to satisfy only himself. In the first case, he has failed to exercise his authority wisely by not using it at all. In the latter, authority has become the job, not a servant to the job as it should be.

When God disciplines His people, He does so in love. "Those whom I love, I reprove and chasten" (Rev. 3:19). So too should the manager use the authority he has. If he is obedient to the command to love others, his decisions will be just, wisely executed and properly used. Whether he is seeking to correct an error or to promote an employee, he must do so in a loving way, considering not himself, but the other people involved.

I recently learned a lesson about using God-given

authority in my job. My staff consists of four teams, each headed by a manager. After I had held the position about six months I determined it was necessary to carefully review the operations of our division and determine how to best utilize our staff. The four team managers and I met often to review the situation and at times the meetings became heated with each man understandably seeking to promote the interests of his staff. My task was to weigh all the facts and my own ideas of the best way to reorganize. At the point when I had all the information I needed to prepare what I felt was a good plan, I could have "pulled rank" on my subordinates by dictating the alternative to be used. Instead, I withheld this use of authority until I could hear the opinions of the team managers and weigh them as impartially as possible. Also, I felt the effect of the changes on the staff would have to be a prime consideration in any decision. I wanted to use existing personnel more effectively but also in a way that would meet their needs. This required a long and tedious process which resulted in some staff changes that were generally acceptable to all concerned. Had I acted on my own initiative I would have made serious errors in assigning people to teams where they would not have been happy. I would have given responsibilities to people not capable of comfortably handling them with their existing work load. Serious problems were avoided by exercising authority God's way.

Commissioned by Christ

The twenty-first chapter of John's Gospel recounts one of Christ's post-resurrection appearances to the disciples. It was at this time that He gave Peter the threefold commission that is applicable today to all who are called to a pastoral ministry. Jesus told Peter, "Feed my lambs. . . . Tend my sheep. . . . Feed my sheep" (John 21:15, 16, 17). In these three short statements the Lord sums up the essence of the pastor's and manager's responsibility toward congregation and staff. This commission comes from Christ; to fail or ignore to carry it out is to reject the direction of God.

It is important that the manager recognize that he is responsible for the flock in his charge. He is responsible for their welfare in regard to the work environment where they have been placed under his authority. To fail to recognize the pastoral responsibility is to be ignorant of the spiritual dimension of the manager's job. He must understand and accept the fact that he is like a shepherd. In doing this he becomes conscious of the commission he has been given, receives it, and begins to act upon it.

9

The Pastor and Manager Contrasted

If the whole body were an eye, where would be the hearing? If the whole body were an ear, where would be the sense of smell? But as it is, God arranged the organs in the body, each one of them, as he chose. If all were a single organ, where would the body be? As it is, there are many parts, yet one body. Now you are the body of Christ and individually members of it. (1 Cor. 12:17-20, 27)

The quotation at the beginning of this chapter is from Paul's famous analogy of the human body and the body of Christ. Through this, the Holy Spirit is teaching us that we are all parts of the body and are all necessary to its proper functioning. We should be aware of what part we are and seek to be perfected in functioning as that part by doing what we are assigned. We should be content to be what God has made us and should not be jealous of another's place or seek to be something we are not. In fact, no matter how hard we try, we will never be capable of performing effectively in a ministry that God has not placed us in but one in which we have placed ourselves.

In the last chapter we showed why management is a ministry and particularly focused on the similarities between management and pastoring. While it is true that the manager is called to be a shepherd, it is equally true that the pastoral ministry of the manager is in many ways different from that of our pastors and priests. It is important that we recognize the similarities and to learn from them, but it is dangerous to try to carry out the management ministry in the same way the pastor of your church carries out his assignment.

The Work Place Is Not a Church

Probably the most serious mistake we can make is to begin to see our work place as a substitute for the church. When we are new in the ways of the Lord it is easy to be so zealous that we want to spend every moment preaching the gospel and leading others to Christ. It is especially tempting for the manager to inadvertently treat his staff as a congregation and to devote all of his time to spiritual matters to the detriment of the work.

The pastor of a church will find his congregation to generally be homogeneous in regard to the common religious beliefs that bring them together. These people come together as a flock to worship God, to study His Word, and to fellowship. Thus, the pastor spends much energy in the spiritual care and feeding of the flock. He evangelizes when it is necessary but spends more of his time tending to spiritual needs and nourishing his flock from the Word of God in order to strengthen them and draw them into a closer relationship with the Lord.

The Christian manager is wrong if he conceives of his staff as a congregation whose primary role is to worship God and fellowship in the Spirit. While there is similarity in that the work day may include prayer, worship and fellowship with some staff members at appropriate times, the two flocks and their functions are different. They must be understood and cared for according to their particular nature. No pastor can lead his congregation like a construction crew and no foreman can treat his crew like a church congregation.

The essential difference is the very reason why each group exists. The body that meets as a church comes together to edify one another and bring glory to God by functioning as the body of Christ. The staff that comes together at the office or factory meets to earn a living through the production and provision of goods and/or services. For the Christian on the staff it is important to approach work with an attitude of using it to God's glory but for the other employees this will not make sense. However, in keeping the right attitude about work the Christian will find that he can worship through his job without having to make worship his work.

Manager or Minister, What Comes First?

The pastor is first and foremost a minister. It is his job. He earns his living by ministering to the spiritual needs of his people. Everything he does is related to and in support of the ministry. His first task is to care for and serve God's people.

In management, the ministry is secondary to the job. The manager's ministry is not his work but grows from the work. The manager's primary concern is to direct his staff in achieving the organization's goals. For the manager, the job is primary. The ministry exists because of the job and complements the management function.

In this chapter we have seen that we should not confuse

the work place with a church. We should apply much of what Scripture teaches to both situations but according to the purpose and nature of the grouping of people. The Christian manager, like the pastor, also wants to lead others to Christ and a closer walk with Him. Unlike the pastor, the manager only does this in the course of carrying out his other tasks; it is not the work his employer is paying him to do.

In the following chapters we will frequently be referring to management as a ministry and to the staff as being a flock. In all cases we will do well to recognize that this analogy to the pastor and his congregation is subject to and limited by the dissimilarities and the similarities of the two situations.

10

The Nature and Needs of the Staff

Then God said, "Let us make man in our image, after
our likeness" . . . So God created man in his own
image, in the image of God he created him; male and
female he created them. (Gen. 1:26, 27)

In the preceding chapters frequent references have
been made to the staff as we have focused on the pastoral
nature of management. It is the staff who have been
entrusted to the care and ministry of the manager.
Whether we manage a shift at a fast-food restaurant, a
crew on an assembly line, or a highly professional group of
administrators and planners, the people who work for us
have the same basic composition and needs. In this
chapter we will consider these people and their needs.

The Composition of the Staff
In order to carry out his responsibility the manager
must be aware of the heterogeneous make-up of his staff
and its impact on his management of them. Whereas the
pastor's flock is relatively homogeneous, the manager's
staff is quite diverse regarding their religious beliefs and

convictions. To simply define this in spiritual terms we can say that the Christian manager's staff is a composite of three categories of people which can be further divided into even smaller groupings. First, there is the *Christian flock* which is composed of the members of the staff that profess Jesus Christ as Savior. This grouping is as varied as the number of denominations represented, the level of each individual's faith, and the degree to which each is submitted to the lordship of Christ. Then, there is the *religious flock* that is made up of those who follow non-Christian religions, belong to various cults or sects like the Jehovah's Witnesses, or are members of Christian denominations but have not received Christ and been born again. Finally, there are those with no religious affiliation including every degree and shade of atheist and agnostic.

As diverse as these groups are they are united as one staff by virtue of a common goal and the common manager. The manager must be able to recognize the similarities and differences of those on his staff. He must know how and when to treat them alike and when to minister to them differently. While the exact methods will differ, he is responsible for carrying out the commission of Christ to the fullest extent possible in each situation.

The Composition of Man

Man is a complex creature, composed of three distinct, yet interrelated, parts: body, soul or mind, and spirit. Most management practices focus on the physical and mental conditions and needs of the men and women who are to be managed and some touch on the emotional welfare of the employee. The books that teach these techniques do an excellent job in that respect but they fail to give any attention to the spiritual dimension of human life. Therefore, we will focus on the spiritual nature and condition of the people who make up the staff.

The quotation from Genesis at the beginning of this chapter stresses that man was created by God in His image. To understand the nature of man or his composition we must first consider what it means to be made in the image of God. In this vein, two ideas will help us.

Man resembles God in that he has been given dominion over creation. God is the maker of all things but He delegated the responsibility to rule over creation to His creature, man. Man lost this dominion to Satan when he sinned, but through the sacrifice of Jesus we can take it once again if we desire it.

To be a capable ruler of something great in value and importance implies several things about the individual. First, man is like God because he is set above the rest of creation. He is like the Creator because he has been given the wisdom he needs to be a ruler. He is like God because he can view creation as good, because he was himself created as good and because God is good. Thus, we are agents of God with a free will that allows us to choose the direction we will take. In this respect man, like God, has a mind of his own and can make decisions. God never forces anything upon us but gives us the opportunity to choose and to direct our own lives.

Since we know that God is spirit we can also see that man was created in His image because of the spirit man possesses. It is this spirit that makes us most like God and makes it possible for us to communicate with the Divine Spirit. Furthermore, as the Spirit of God directs and controls the universe, our human spirits were made to be the controlling and directing part of us. While this was the purpose of God putting His breath into us (Gen. 2:7) and making us spiritual beings, we do not always leave our spirit in charge but allow other parts of our being to be in control.

These other parts are the body and soul (or mind). The body is the physical and animal-like nature of man. Representative of this part of man are the various appetites such as hunger and the sex drive. The soulish nature is the intellectual center of man. It is the rational and decision-making part and the seat of the emotions. It is with the soul that man establishes values and makes moral judgments.

In summary, man is most like God because he too is a spirit. But man, as spirit, lives in a body and possesses a soul. These three natures compete with one another to dominate a person's existence. It is to the relationship between them that we now turn our attention.

Spiritual Condition

Man is essentially good. This may seem to be a questionable assertion when one considers the violence, crime, hatred and other sin that pervades the world, but it is nonetheless true. God, being good, could not make anything less than perfect. "And God saw everything that he had made, and behold, it was very good" (Gen. 1:31).

Though man was created good he chose to disobey God and thus brought sin into the world. Sin does not only affect the sinner but, like the shock waves of an earthquake, it can give birth to a tidal wave, causing multiple repercussions. We can look around us and see that our sins always touch others, leading to more sin. If we lie to someone we can be sure the lie will return to us, causing us to lie again to cover up the first lie, generating misunderstanding, leading to anger and all that follows. Man's first disobedience had the same sort of effect. Sin was loosed in the world and man, being born into the world, is immersed in sin. The way a person chooses to respond to the corruption of the world is the determining factor in his or her spiritual condition.

The spiritual condition of a person is characterized by the extent of the spirit's dominance over his bodily and soulish natures and the direction to which the spirit is turned (i.e. to self, to God, to Satan, or to the world).

A man can be controlled by any of his three natures and the choice is his. In the lives of even the most mature Christians there are times when the flesh or the mind can overrule the desire of our spirit and control our actions. Even Paul, God's pious servant, had to deal with this as the following passage shows.

> I don't understand myself at all, for I really want to do what is right, but I can't. I do what I don't want to—what I hate. I know perfectly well that what I am doing is wrong, and my bad conscience proves that I agree with these laws I am breaking. But I can't help myself, because I'm no longer doing it. It is sin inside me that is stronger than I am that makes me do these evil things. (Rom. 7:15-17 TLB)

> So you see how it is: my new life tells me to do right, but the old nature that is still inside me loves to sin. Oh, what a terrible predicament I'm in! Who will free me from my slavery to this deadly lower nature? Thank God! It has been done by Jesus Christ our

Lord. He has set me free. (Rom. 7:24-25 TLB)

What Paul is lamenting about here is the condition we all find ourselves in when other than a God-focused spirit gives us directions.

As managers we must seek to understand what happens when the different natures are in primary control. Without some insight into this we will be hampered in our ministry to others.

When the physical nature directs someone, he or she is, in biblical language, living according to the flesh, allowing the desires and lusts of the flesh to dictate what they do. It is clear that when the flesh exercises control, sin cannot be avoided. "Now the works of the flesh are plain: immorality, impurity, licentiousness, idolatry, sorcery, enmity, strife, jealousy, anger, selfishness, dissension, party spirit, envy, drunkenness, carousing, and the like" (Gal. 5:19-21).

When the mind is dominant it is possible to intellectually assent to the teachings of Christ but unless this is fed through the spirit, the individual will rely on his or her own understanding and wisdom. This results in the doctrines of those like the Pharisees who sought salvation through strict observance of *their* interpretation of the Law. The Bible cautions us about the mind-controlled person:

For there are many insubordinate men, empty talkers and deceivers, especially the circumcision party; they must be silenced, since they are upsetting whole families by teaching for base gain what they have no right to teach. . . . To the pure all things are pure, but to the corrupt and unbelieving nothing is pure; their very minds and consciences are corrupted. They profess to know God, but they deny him by their deeds; they are detestable, disobedient, unfit for any good deed. (Titus 1:10-11, 15-16)

When a man chooses to be directed by his physical and/or soulish nature he generally will be following the way of the world, satisfying his appetites and natural inquisitiveness with that which seems good to him. By placing his spirit in submission to his other natures a man cannot know nor understand the ways of God.

For many years I allowed my intellect and my flesh to guide me. Even when I attended church or read the Scriptures, I could not comprehend the truth when I was faced with it. God's ways made no sense to me. Then, when I realized my need for Jesus and was baptized in the Holy Spirit, I began to see the folly of the world and to understand God's way of living. My spiritual eyes were opened and the ears of my inner man were unstopped. Because I opened my spirit to God I could communicate with Him, and because I let my spirit take charge, God's Spirit began to control my flesh and my mind so that they could be purged and transformed into the person of Christ.

The spirit of Jesus was so perfectly attuned to the Holy Spirit that His every action, His every thought was an expression of the will of God. This is the way we originally were and are meant to be.

A word of caution is needed here. Simply allowing the inner man or spirit to control does not bring about a transformation like the one just shared. It is that to which we turn our spirit's attention that is the critical factor. When the spirit is in control we are necessarily opening it to other influences in the spiritual world by searching for something to which the spirit can relate. If we look inward to ourselves, with or without the help of drugs or other mind-altering experiences, or if we turn outside of ourselves toward the occult, using tarot cards, astrology and the like, we are baring our inner being to the influence of Satan and his demons. This is why the spiritual experiences associated with the use of drugs or mind-control techniques are so dangerous. There is only one way to turn our spirit toward God and that is by making Jesus our Savior and Lord. "Jesus said to him, 'I am the way, and the truth, and the life; no one comes to the Father, but by me' " (John 14:6).

What happens when we have directed our spirit godward and subjected our other natures to the spiritual nature? God's Holy Spirit communes with our spirit and begins to work in us to create a new creature. We grow in the fruit of the Christ-life and begin the transformation of our entire being into the perfection of Jesus.

This has been a brief and simplified treatment of a subject that is complicated and deserving of much deeper and comprehensive consideration. This overview has been presented here, because it is essential that the manager understand something about man's nature, so that he is able to assess the spiritual condition of his employees in order to make it possible to identify and meet their spiritual needs.

Spiritual Needs
The body, the mind, and the spirit all have certain essential requirements that must be met if they are to remain healthy. These include proper nourishment, exercise and hygiene. In this section we will discuss some

basic spiritual needs and the effect that a lack of attention to them can have on the person's ability to do his best work. In a later section we will look at some ways the manager can help meet these needs.

The God Experience. Man was made to commune with God and until his disobedience created the gulf between the Creator and the creature, man was in perfect communion with Him. This gap, created by sin, has been bridged by Jesus Christ. But to cross the bridge each person must desire to turn to God. Unless a man can experience the presence of God he will never find true peace and joy. Charles Colson made it to the top of the legal profession and was a key advisor to President Richard Nixon. Yet he admits that until he turned to Christ, his life was empty despite his success.

To have a personal relationship with God through Jesus is the first spiritual need that must be met in a person's life. Unless an individual can turn to God and fellowship with Him, his or her life cannot be in order; either the flesh, the mind or Satan will be in control and the person will not experience the gentle direction of the Holy Spirit.

How does this affect a person's work? Most simply, he or she will lack the peace of Christ. They may be restless, rebellious, hard to get along with, troubled about many problems, lacking a desire to do well, or so centered on work that they fail to be considerate of others, including their own family. In essence, they will be unbalanced in their spirits. From this unbalanced condition any number of problems can arise for the manager.

As the manager grows more mature in ministry and learns to discern the spiritual condition of others this need becomes relatively easy to recognize. However, it cannot be met once and considered fulfilled. Man's need to walk with God is ever continuing.

We all experience days when we feel cut off from God, and unless we are careful we soon find ourselves anxious, rebellious and confused. Man needs to be in constant communion with God. That is why Jesus came and sent the Holy Spirit to dwell in us. The need to experience God is never fully satisfied but varies in degrees from those who have had no relationship with Him, to those who have walked with Him daily for a lifetime but who experience brief moments when they feel alone.

Moral Direction. Moral decisions, that is, judgments which distinguish good from evil, are made in the mind. However, the direction, the intuition—that which impresses on the mind the proper course of action, that which provides the intangible measure for all we do, that which may be called conscience—is a spiritual need all men have. It is the Holy Spirit who teaches us right from wrong. "But the Counselor, the Holy Spirit, whom the Father will send in my name, he will teach you all things, and bring to your remembrance all that I have said to you" (John 14:26). And, God's Spirit teaches us through our spirits.

Men who are controlled by their minds can live a good moral life but without the Spirit of truth teaching them in their inner man they can never understand that to deny Christ is disobedience and self-pride. Therefore, to receive this moral direction one must be turned godward.

If we are not receiving the Spirit's guidance or are ignoring it, our relationships with others may be strained, leading to strife and creating an uncomfortable working environment. This lack of direction can also lead to self-centered pride which results in the individual working to improve his or her position at the expense of the organization and others.

In order to live a life of love for others, a life in which relationships are not strained and people are compatible, a person's spirit must be open to receive direction from God that will provide a basis for taking action and making decisions. Love is seeking the well-being of others and this cannot be achieved unless we are obedient to God.

Death and Beyond: The Future Certainty. All men are interested in their future. All know that ultimately they will die but many are unsure what, if anything, happens after death. To know what to expect at death and after is a spiritual need. It is a need that can only be met through faith in Jesus and the reality of His death and resurrection. He promises, "For this is the will of my Father, that every one who sees the Son and believes in him should have eternal life; and I will raise him up at the last day" (John 6:40). Without Jesus, no one can have certainty about what lies beyond death. There are theories, thoughts, wishes, but not one can guarantee eternal life except the One who overcame death.

Before I knew Christ I was never sure what would happen to me when I died. Each time I did something I knew was wrong I wondered if I could be forgiven. I questioned if there was life after death and I feared death, for I knew I would have to face it but had no hope, no assurance of life beyond the grave. I more or less held that there was some sort of heaven and that all men who believed in God (not Christ) would go there because God would not need to create a hell with our sinful, trial-filled earth.

Inside I felt that there was something more than a few years on earth but I did not know what. This uncertainty about my future was part of the overall uncertainty I experienced about my life because I could see no ultimate goal to anything I did. Career, family, nothing could be placed in perspective when the perspective was hazy and unstable.

This instability affected my relationships with others both at work and elsewhere. If life was just a passing thing I could only treat others as just passing through my life with no concrete purpose beyond the immediate conversation or recreation.

Then I met Jesus and my future life for all eternity was assured. A goal was firmly established—to do all I could in service to the Lord before He took me home. I know that nothing that happens to me here can alter what has been promised to me. Therefore, I am free to follow Jesus, to do His will knowing that the ultimate goal of my life is guaranteed. I am no longer in competition with others but I want to help them come to know Christ. I am no longer anxious about career or family because I know that the Lord will provide and care for us. I am, at last, at peace; and able to look beyond myself to others, to be fulfilled not by gaining prestige or fame, but by following Jesus and loving those whom He sends to me.

The need is for peace and certainty about the future. Without it nothing is stable about life. Without this peace life is filled with anxiety and worry about the future. It is a life in which nothing satisfies.

Spiritual Nourishment. As the body needs nourishment, so does the spirit. The body requires food to grow, to remain healthy, to fight off illness, to be strong, to heal after an injury. Spiritual food is required by the spirit for analogous reasons. By spiritual nourishment we mean the Word of God, testimonies to God's glory and power, hearing and studying about God and our life with Him, and communing with the Lord regularly in prayer.

When we are immersed in God's love and the things of His love we are spiritually nourished. If we receive the proper feeding, our spirits will be strong enough to resist Satan, and should we receive a spiritual hurt, it will be able to heal rapidly.

Just as we can fill the body with "junk" foods that have little or no value as nourishment, the spirit can also be fed "junk." If the spirit is saturated with the things of this world—violent television shows, pornography, filthy language, off-color jokes, and the like—it will be fed but not nourished. A spirit stuffed with useless and harmful things is weak. It does not grow close to God but slips away and when attacked it has no strength for defense.

What the spirit is fed is what the spirit has to feed others. If a person lives a life filled with sensuousness, he will bring his lust and all that goes with it to the work place. If cursing is received by his spirit, cursing will come forth in the office. If an individual's spirit is weak and fed sinful things, this iniquity, this proclivity to do wrong, will come to work with the person.

Spiritual Exercise. For the spiritual nature of a person to remain strong and in control, it must be exercised. The spirit is like a muscle that will atrophy if it is not used. It is exercised in fellowship, service and ministry. Just as one's spirit is fed by the Christ-centered fellowship of others, one tones the muscle of his spirit by sharing the Lord, by giving of himself. If the inner man is ill-nourished and has nothing good to give, it will not be exercised. A weak spirit is soon dominated by the flesh and/or the mind.

Faith

Above we identified five categories of man's spiritual needs but we did not discuss how the manager can go about helping to meet them. The central requirement of the satisfaction of these needs is *faith*, and the manager must first help to build up the faith of his staff before he can minister to specific needs. Without faith a man cannot turn toward God; without faith a man cannot open his spirit to the moral guidance of the Holy Spirit; without faith a man cannot believe that he has been guaranteed eternal life; without faith a spirit will reject wholesome nourishment that it needs, and will not step out in fellowship or ministry.

"Now faith is the assurance of things hoped for, the conviction of things not seen" (Heb. 11:1). Assurance means that there is a guarantee, and conviction means that there is certainty. This means that though you cannot see the object of faith, you *know* that it is there. The essence of faith, then, is to live by trusting God. It is living according to His Word which says, "I will never fail you nor forsake you" (Heb. 13:5).

A manager cannot impart faith to another, for faith is a gift that only can be given by God. But, he can help bring others to a point where they will recognize their need for the gift and he can help to build the faith of his staff. Through this process the manager ministers to the spiritual needs of his employees.

Building Faith

We help to build the faith of others (1) through example;

(2) by sharing God's Word; (3) through testimony and witness; (4) in prayer; and (5) through personal ministry. In all this the manager should remember that the primary task is not to minister but to manage a producing staff. Therefore, any ministry should only be pursued as a part of the job and not in place of it.

Living Example. We have already alluded to the importance of being a good example to the staff and one of the primary reasons is to build up and encourage their faith. In the fourth chapter of Romans the writer uses the example of Abraham's faith and holds it up to all future generations. He says, "Abraham believed God, and it was reckoned to him as righteousness" (Rom. 4:3).

The example of Abraham shows us what it means to live by faith. Do you worry about paying the bills? Are you anxious about landing a contract? Or do you trust all such matters to God, believing in His promise to care for you? Simply live either way without any signposts and your staff will soon discern just how much faith you have. Have you ever read a testimony about how someone relied on God who saw him through trouble to prosperity? If you did, it built your faith, it may have led you to say to yourself, "If God could work so great a miracle for him, He can do it for me!" Live a life that openly reflects your trust in God and give Him the glory when He takes you over the rough spots and brings you success.

Sharing God's Word. "So faith comes from what is heard, and what is heard comes by the preaching of Christ" (Rom. 10:17). God's Word can reach the spirit of a person through all the muck and mire that the world deposits as a barrier. "For the word of God is living and active, sharper than any two-edged sword, piercing to the division of soul and spirit, of joints and marrow, and discerning the thoughts and intentions of the heart" (Heb. 4:12).

In order to build up the faith of others, managers should learn to freely use the Word of God as a normal reference point in any situation. To do so effectively we must be familiar with what is contained between the covers of the Bible. This does not mean that the Word should be carelessly bandied about but that it should be applied wherever possible and when necessary.

In addition to having a Bible study in my office, I find that as I become more and more immersed in the Word, I openly apply God's teaching to all types of situations, varying from personnel decisions to choosing office equipment. My philosophy has become, "If God said it, it is true, and if it is applicable we had better heed it." This sharing of the Scripture is not planned or forced, it just comes naturally as a by-product of my spirit's nourishment by the Word. Jesus told us that what comes out of a man's mouth is from the heart and if we are filled with God's Word then it will come forth like a clear running stream.

Many things can happen when you use the Word like this. Some will completely tune you out. Usually, though, when it is applied in a business discussion or when a person is asking you a question that relates to your walk with the Lord, it is heard and internalized by the hearer. After sharing a Scripture with others I have even heard non-Christians going about their business quoting what I had spoken to them! When people are exposed to the Word of God it is loosed to do its work of building faith.

Testimony and Witness. Sharing your testimony about what God has done for you and witnessing to His love, mercy and power is a part of living the example of faith and sharing God's Word.

In giving your testimony you are telling others that God can do even greater things in their lives and thus you build up their faith. When we strengthen faith, we have a part in the ultimate defeat of the enemy of faith. There is truly much strength in testimony to be imparted to those who hear it.

Prayer. Prayer should undergird all of our efforts to nurture faith. We must be obedient to the Scripture which exhorts us to offer prayers for all men at all times.

In prayer we can ask the Lord to build the faith of our employees, to meet their needs, to solve their problems, to bring them closer to Him. In prayer we admit that we cannot help them ourselves but that we need the Lord to do it. At the same time we can open ourselves to be vessels for the Lord's use in ministry to our staff. Our prayer should also include requests for discernment so that we may understand the spiritual condition of those who concern us, for knowledge that will enable us to identify their needs, for wisdom to show us how to minister to them, and for grace to enable us to carry out that ministry.

Personal Ministry. There are often times that the less direct ministries we have discussed will not touch the specific problem area or meet the precise need of an individual. Such a situation may require the manager to enter into a personal ministry of regular, planned counseling and prayer sessions that are designed to help the employee deal with a problem or a series of related needs. Before becoming fully committed to this ministry with an employee, the manager would do well to pray about it to discern whether the Lord is actually leading him to do the ministering. Such a ministry can be difficult and, if it is not in the Lord's plan or if He wants someone else to do it, it will be a frustrating and impossible task. Therefore, it is wise to ask the Lord to provide someone to minister and to make it clear through circumstances and your inner witness as to who is to do it.

If summoned to enter into such a ministry the manager will use the same methods we have already discussed but in more concentrated form and directed to the specific problem. For example, if you are ministering to the Christian wife of a nonbeliever who is considering divorce, you would want to use the appropriate Scriptures that deal with husband-wife relationships; you would share what the Lord has done in your marriage and encourage the person to continue to trust the Lord. For someone with a drinking problem you will tailor the ministry to the need. In all cases, keep the ministry supported by your prayers and the prayers of other Christians.

All of these methods help to meet spiritual needs by demonstrating the reality and power of God, His love and His mercy. These things help others to believe and open them to the working of the Holy Spirit who imparts the gift of faith which brings them to the assurance and peace of salvation.

To be able to use these methods effectively the manager must be constantly aware of the nature and needs of those who make up his staff. Like a shepherd must know all he can about his sheep if he is to care for them properly, the manager must understand the spiritual nature of his people if he is to effectively serve them in ministry.

11

A Relationship
Built on Love

And as you wish that men would do to you, do so to
them. (Luke 6:31)

No man lives alone and untouched by others. Even the
hermit who has turned his back on society has been
shaped and formed in his contact with others. The very
decision to live in seclusion is arrived at because of the
way the hermit related to others. We cannot ignore the
importance of relationships between individuals. Most of
our personality, our beliefs, our goals, and our dreams are
formed by the network of relationships that make up our
lives. The influence of parents, siblings, friends, teachers,
of anyone who has touched our lives, can easily be
recognized. The acknowledgment of this fact is important
to gaining an understanding of the nature of our ties to
others.

The way we relate to one another is grounded in the
bond between the individual and Christ. If a person is not
following Jesus the resulting lack of direction and true
peace will negatively influence his dealings with other
people. Jesus made it plain that all relationships were to

be subservient to our walk with Him when He said, "If any one comes to me and does not hate his own father and mother and wife and children and brothers and sisters, yes, even his own life, he cannot be my disciple" (Luke 14:26). This does not mean we are to hate or despise others in the sense that we do not love them, but that we are to recognize that Jesus comes first in our lives. Unless this is a fact in each individual's life he or she will never be able to have proper relations with others. By putting our union with the Lord in its proper place all of our other ties will become ordered as a part of that primary relationship.

We have already dealt with the manager's walk with Christ. Now we will focus on how the manager relates to his employees. Since our contacts with others play such a major role in our lives, the Scriptures abound with guidance we need to learn and apply in order to live and work together. Here we will sample this wisdom and apply it to the practice of management.

A Word on Relationships

The formation of interpersonal relationships is essentially influenced by the way we perceive one another. As two people spend time together, at work, at play, in fellowship, in simply discussing the weather, each makes numerous conscious and unconscious observations about the other. These observations combine in the observer's mind to form an image or perception that is the sum of what he believes about the other's likes, dislikes, habits, etc. The way we respond and behave around one another is largely dictated by this perception. If I perceive my boss as a strict, business-always type, I will not believe it to be beneficial or perhaps even possible to spend the time telling him about the new baby or my vacation. If, on the other hand, I see a warm, compassionate individual who is interested in more than my contribution to company profits, I will freely share these parts of my life with him. In this instance my relationship with my boss is dictated by what I perceive to be his attitude toward me, and this perception shows me how to respond. Furthermore, the essence of the response is the decision to reveal or conceal certain aspects of self. The more we expose our personality to others the closer we get to them and this affinity grows because of the other's receptiveness toward us, otherwise we probably would not reveal these things. Thus in a solid marriage we will find nothing secret between husband and wife. In the same way, the openness with which the manager and his staff share their lives will influence the strength of the bond between them.

When all relationships are centered in Christ, God's way of seeing others becomes our perception of them. We begin to see Christ in other believers and respond to them as we would to Jesus. We are able to look at nonbelievers as God's children who have gone astray but who are greatly loved by their Father and should be so loved by us. We must learn to recognize each person's need for love that is of God. Thus, all of our relationships must be grounded in love. The way we are and respond toward others must be motivated by the same love that led Jesus to give himself for us.

The Staff's Perception of the Manager

The way employees view the manager and therefore their relationship with that manager, will be greatly affected by the life they see him living. The dedicated, hard-working but loving manager will show this in all his actions, generally causing his people to respond in an equally loving and dedicated fashion.

The manager must be respected by his staff for his professional competence and he must be respected for his authority. Moreover, the manager must have the esteem of his staff as a fair and honest individual who treats them with respect and compassion.

Secondly, the employees must recognize the manager as a leader. By definition every manager is a leader but to actually be accepted as such is a different thing. If he is not held in high regard by his staff the manager will not be able to function as a leader whom the staff is willing to follow. We see Jesus as someone who will guide us along the best path. We are able to trust and follow Him without hesitation. The manager must have the confidence of his employees. Men will stay with a leader through all situations when they believe he knows what he is doing. The same men will be quick to abandon one they believe to be incompetent. A manager's leadership ability can be measured by response to his direction. If he is respected and trusted by his staff, they will willingly receive his directions.

The staff must respond to the manager as an authority. Again, we know that a person who is placed in a position of authority is not necessarily recognized as such by others. Unless the employees know they can receive valid direction, instruction and advice from their boss, they will not easily accept his exercise of authority. If the staff does not perceive the manager as being capable of doing his job they will be reluctant to follow his directions and seek to circumvent them whenever possible. Before a manager is recognized as an authority he must demonstrate that he is, in fact, an authority.

Finally, employees must be able to trust the manager. They must believe he has their welfare at heart and desires what is best for them. If he is trusted, he will find his employees free to counsel with him. They will be eager to offer suggestions and open to advice. Trust forms the basis for both respect of the manager and the perception of his leadership role.

The manager must be trusted, viewed with respect, accepted as a leader and recognized as an authority by his staff if he is to be effective. The staff's perception of the manager is prescribed by the example he sets in his work and life and by the way he treats them.

The Manager's Perception of the Staff

The various management schools discussed in chapter three present several ways in which a manager can view his employees. The perception he has of them is critical to the way he chooses to treat those who work for him. If he conceives of his staff people as being basically lazy he will push them to produce. If he believes they are greedy he will hold out the carrot of economic reward in order to motivate them. The way the manager comes to understand his employees influences the development of his management style.

Basic to the formation of a proper attitude toward staff is the understanding that he is not a more superior person than those over whom he is placed. This is because all those who work for him have the same Father as he even if they do not recognize it. The essence of this relationship is summed up in the following quote from Scripture: "Don't just pretend that you love others: really love them. Hate what is wrong. Stand on the side of the good. Love each other with brotherly affection and take delight in honoring each other" (Rom. 12:9-10 TLB).

In recognizing the brotherhood he has in common with the employees, the manager accepts also responsibility and authority in order to serve them. He must approach his flock with the attitude that he has such a great responsibility for them that he should be willing to even lay down his life for them.

In sum, we cannot see ourselves as better than our employees. Just because we hold a position of authority over them does not make us superior persons. Like them, we are sinners in need of God's mercy. Like them, we are children of God. By recognizing this we are more capable of lovingly ministering to the needs of the staff as a servant to his master, while, at the same time, overseeing them in the performance of their tasks. Any other perception will lead the manager away from the model Christ provided as the Good Shepherd and will result in management based on the world's rather than divine wisdom.

Caring

The manager's perception of his employees contributes to his care for them while his treatment of them, in turn, influences his perception. The way he approaches the staff is probably the single most important factor in the formation of the employee's perception of the manager. Treatment, perception, all facets of the relationship, are bound up in the practical application of the principles of Christian management.

"Don't be selfish; don't live to make a good impression on others. Be humble, thinking of others as better than yourself. Don't just think about your own affairs, but be interested in others, too, and in what they are doing" (Phil. 2:3-4 TLB). This should be the manager's attitude toward the staff. He must care for them! In an excellent book, Milton Mayeroff shares the following insights about *caring*.

> To care for another person, in the most significant sense, is to help him grow and actualize himself.
>
> Caring is the antithesis of simply using the other person to satisfy one's own needs.
>
> Caring, as helping another grow and actualize himself, is a process, a way of relating to someone that involves development, in the same way that friendship can only emerge in time through mutual trust and a deepening and qualitative transformation of the relationship.[1]

The caring defined by Mayeroff is a natural outflow when we practice Christ's command to love one another as He loved us (John 15:12). It springs from the selfless love that is most interested in the welfare of the other person, their growth and development. Whatever is done in the relationship is done for the one cared for. A child who plays with matches will be spanked, not to hurt the child but because it is for the child's well-being to learn not to play with matches. Likewise, it is for the good of the employee and those he works with that a manager scolds and even suspends a worker for unsafely using a piece of equipment.

The Manager's Care

The manager's care for his staff is evidenced in trust,

[1]Milton Mayeroff, *On Caring* (Harper and Row, Publishers: New York, 1971), p. 1.

patience, and most of all, in his kindness toward them.

We can never truly express our care for another person unless we develop an ability to trust him. If the manager constantly controls his staff, dictating every last detail of the task to be accomplished, he will create a group of dependent robots. If he trusts employees with increasingly responsible assignments he creates an atmosphere in which the individual can grow and mature. Unless he trusts his employees, the manager cannot know their strengths and weaknesses and cannot know the best way to guide them for themselves and the organization. While it is at times difficult to extend trust, it is necessary. "Trusting the other is to let go; it includes an element of risk and a leap into the unknown, both of which take courage."[2] Such a leap and such courage are essential to healthy perceptions on both sides of the relationship.

Patience is a fruit of the Holy Spirit and is a particularly desirable quality in a manager. Paul exhorts us to extend this patience to all people. "And we exhort you brethren, admonish the idle, encourage the fainthearted, help the weak, be patient with them all" (1 Thess. 5:14).

We tend to think of patience as something inactive but Mayeroff points out that this is a misconception. "Patience is not waiting passively for something to happen, but is a kind of participation with the other in which we give fully of ourselves."[3]

This is the kind of patience that God has with us. If He did nothing but wait for us to grow we would never move. Instead, He works with us, guides us, counsels us toward the goal He has established for us. He is patient in that He does not expect us to grow rapidly or to reach our objective immediately. He knows we will falter and at

[2]Ibid., p. 21.
[3]Ibid., p. 17.

140

times slip backward, yet He is always there to help us.
This kind of enduring patience is most expressive of
care. Unless we care for someone very much it is
impossible to work with them as Jesus does with us. The
patience that the manager has with his employees must
recognize strengths and weaknesses and adjust to them.
It is a patience that is more concerned with attaining the
long-term goal of growth than a less important immediate
objective.

Kindness is characteristic of every sort of caring. The
manager expresses kindness toward the staff by always
being available to help with difficulties or to share in
victories. As the kindness of God endures forever, so the
kindness of the Christian must be constant and
never-ending. A gentle word of encouragement, a calm
and helpful correction, special allowances made to aid a
person in a difficult situation, these are all examples of the
kindness that should characterize the manager's
relationship with those who work for him.

Rough, unloving treatment will create an atmosphere
of distrust and anxiety, and will widen the gap between
manager and employee. Kind, caring treatment will
overcome anxiety and will draw the manager into a closer
communion with his staff. "Kindness makes a man
attractive" (Prov. 19:22 TLB).

Caring Is Loving

We have defined love as being a free giving of oneself
for the sake of another, of placing the other's needs and
desires ahead of one's own, of desiring good for the other.
How do we exhibit this love for one another? We know it is
not enough to only express our love with words and in
feelings. We know that as Jesus' love for us was made

manifest in His ministry to us, we are to manifest our love toward others by the things we do for them. What, then, are the characteristics of love that are exemplified in our actions toward others?

In search of an answer we turn to the thirteenth chapter of Paul's first letter to the Corinthians which is often referred to as the "love chapter." It is here that we find the fullest description of Christ-like love that is to be found in the Bible.

Love is patient and kind; love is not jealous or boastful; it is not arrogant or rude. Love does not insist on its own way; it is not irritable or resentful; it does not rejoice at wrong, but rejoices in the right. Love bears all things, believes all things, hopes all things, endures all things.

Love never ends; as for prophecies, they will pass away; as for tongues, they will cease; as for knowledge, it will pass away. (1 Cor. 13:4-8)

Each characteristic listed is an element of Christ's love for us. In imitation we should show forth these attributes in our love for our brothers and sisters, including those at work. The manager does well to carefully study this and learn its application. In the remainder of this chapter we will reflect on the meaning of this characterization of love and suggest some application of it to the manager's ministry.

Love Is Patient

How patient is God's love for us? How many times did the Israelites stray from their Lord yet were always received by Him when they returned? How often have each of us acted out our version of the Parable of the Prodigal Son and found that the Lord was waiting for us with His arms wide open? God's patience is exemplified in that "the Son of man came to seek and to save the lost" (Luke 19:10).

Are you patient with your employees? If one of your people cannot seem to understand how to decorate the store window do you patiently explain over again how it is to be done? Do you offer encouragement or do you throw up your hands in despair and do it yourself, mumbling under your breath about the quality of help?

Patient love is understanding love, slow to anger and quick to forgive. It looks beyond the weaknesses of the other that tend to irritate and ministers to them while focusing on their strong points. Patience requires gentle guidance at the pace of the employee and attuned to that person's ability.

Love Is Kind

In His kindness God has given us everything we need to live an abundant life on earth and an everlasting life with Him in His kingdom. According to His example, God has asked us to feed the hungry, provide drink for the thirsty, greet the stranger, clothe the naked, visit the sick, and go to the prisoner (Matt. 25:34-40). How often have we ignored the physical and spiritual needs of our co-workers or our staff? In time of special need have you extended an extra consideration, such as allowing time off? Have you offered help away from the office, a ride to the doctor's or a visit to the hospital? Have you ever bothered to get your secretary a cup of coffee in the morning rather than sending her to get you one?

Acts of kindness are ways of expressing our desire for the good of another. Look for ways you can show kindness to those you work with. It may be a word of encouragement, the offer of a prayer for a need, a word to notice a new tie, or taking your secretary out to lunch on her birthday. The specific act is not so important, what is important is the heartfelt desire to serve the other person.

Love Is Not Jealous
Jealousy is a self-controlled emotion that has no place in love. The concern we show for our boss so that we will be "on his good list" is bred of jealousy and not love. The disciple's love is not jealous. It seeks the good of the other and rejoices in the blessings given the person loved. Love is not to be concerned with the good you will receive from it but for the good you can do for someone else. We do not love our employees in order to keep them on our side or to make producing workers out of them. We love our staff because they are our brothers and sisters and are deserving of our love.

Love Is Not Boastful or Arrogant
If we truly love others we do not boast of the things we have accomplished or of the good that has come our way. Love realizes that we have nothing worth more than that which is available to anyone else through Christ Jesus. To boast is to be proud, to place ourselves first.

To be arrogant is to consider yourself better than anyone else, it is conceit. Love does not do this, it considers others to be worth more than self and seeks to come to their assistance. Love wilts and dies in self-pride and blossoms in humility.

The manager must be humble in his love for his staff. If he is condescending he will never really understand their needs. Unless the manager places himself on an equal level with his employees, he is not capable of ministering to them as he should because by considering himself above them, he cannot obtain an accurate assessment of their needs. The old Indian proverb that you should walk a mile in someone else's moccasins before criticizing them holds true for the manager as well.

Love Is Not Rude

Love is considerate. In love you never insist on your own rights because you are the boss or expert. The manager exercises this aspect of love by listening to the suggestions, complaints and comments of his employees, by seeking to use the contributions of the staff, and giving credit to those working for him for a job well done. The manager knows that his success is directly attributable to the ability of his employees and he is sure to see that recognition is given even though, by virtue of his authority, he could take the credit for himself. Again, he does not place his own well-being ahead of others'.

Love Is Not Selfish

The unselfish nature of Jesus reached its zenith when He gave up His divinity to humbly die for us. To lay down our lives is to give ourselves for the good of someone else. This is what the manager is called to do by virtue of his discipleship. He is not to carry out his managerial responsibility and minister to his staff for his own benefit, but for those whom he works with, to the glory of God. The manager is to imitate Christ and give himself for his employees.

Love Is Not Irritable
All individuals have different habits and ways of doing
the same things. It is not unusual for the way we do
something, or act, or talk to cause a problem for someone
else. Love looks beyond the difficulty and at Jesus in the
person. When you live in love you will not be angered by
the fact that you are late for an appointment because the
draftsperson who used your car forgot to get gasoline.
You recognize that the mistake is a part of the general
fallibility of the human race that you are also susceptible
to. You do not let minor annoyances flare up into angry
lectures or disciplinary actions.

At the same time, you seek to act toward others in a
fashion that is not disagreeable to them. You respect their
freedom and do not impose your own opinions on them.
Rather than presenting a matter to someone in a way that
might cause anger, seek the most gentle way, the way
that will not upset the other. Seek to be neither irritable
nor irritating.

Love Is Not Resentful
In His infinite love God has forgiven all our sins through
the atoning death of Jesus. Like the woman at the well
and the woman caught in adultery, we are forgiven our
sins. God has promised, "I will forgive their iniquity, and I
will remember their sin no more" (Jer. 31:34). This should
teach us that it is wrong to hold grudges or to be resentful
about anything anyone does to us. Love is forgiving and
understanding. "Above all hold unfailing your love for one
another, since love covers a multitude of sins" (1 Pet. 4:8).

Whenever we sin and repent, God no longer sees our sin
but our soul cleansed by the blood of His Son. Because He

loves us so much to forgive us and forget our sins He continues to pour out His blessings and graces upon us. Past sins that have been forgiven do nothing to hinder our communion with the Lord.

When an employee does something wrong, our forgiveness for that person is as important as the correction or disciplinary action that is necessary. By forgiving we loose the employee of the burden of his error. If we fail to release him like this we soon find ourselves in the position of unfairly evaluating present performance on the basis of past failures.

Thus a basic part of love is to quickly forgive the faults and failings of others so they may be free to receive God's grace that is imparted through us to strengthen them to overcome these difficulties. This does not mean overlooking the wrong but that once it is brought to light and corrected it is to be forgotten and the slate is to be wiped clean.

Love Rejoices in Right

To approve or look away from the sins of someone is not to love that person. Rather, the person who sins should be gently corrected. True love is love that disciplines and corrects the wrongdoer. To allow a sinner to continue in sin is to leave him in the hands of Satan. To make him aware of his sin and the forgiveness he can find in Christ is to love the sinner while hating the sin.

Rejoice in that which is right and good. Put your full support behind those who dwell in the truth even when it is unpopular to do so. The sin which you stand against may be a favorite, like gossip in the office, and to be against it may earn jeers and other persecution. But, it is in love for the sinner that we will suffer as we stand for the truth. To do otherwise is to allow spiritual sickness and death to attack those around us.

Love Bears All Things

Nothing destroys love. Though God's chosen people, Israel, reject Jesus as the Messiah, God does not withdraw His love from them. They are His children despite their rejection. Salvation is still theirs: "A hardening has come upon part of Israel, until the full number of the Gentiles come in, and so all Israel will be saved" (Rom. 11:25-26).

If this rejection of God's own Son did not destroy His love for Israel, how can any petty human disagreement be allowed to cause one's love for another to turn cold? Nothing can be allowed to reduce the love you have for your brothers and sisters. Relations may be strained at times, but they should never be broken. Genuine love will not fall victim to the attacks of Satan no matter how concentrated his effort against us.

Love Believes All Things

Jesus had unlimited and unfailing faith in the Father. He loved Him and knew He was loved by God. In a relationship founded on love only good can be expected. Love leaves no room for doubt about motives. It provides no opportunity for suspicion, for probing or prying.

When you were a child you knew your mother loved you and you did not doubt that the food she prepared for you was good. Though you may have disliked the vegetables, you never believed that she would give you poison. When you show love to those whom you work with they know they can trust you to have their best interest in mind. When authority is founded on love it is easier for others to accept it. If God was unloving we would resent His authority rather than rejoice in the good that comes from it. Love leaves no room to doubt your motives and makes for a more open and honest relationship with those you share your life with.

Love Has Unlimited Hope

Love is always optimistic. Rather than looking at the bad in a situation, love seeks and focuses on the good. Love knows the meaning of the Spirit's promise that "We know that in everything God works for good with those who love him, who are called according to his purpose" (Rom. 8:28). No matter how bleak it may appear on the surface, love always sees the bright side of a situation. When we love someone we can look past those things we dislike and see that which is given by God. With love we can see one another with God's eyes, as helpless children in need of mercy and comfort. Love gives us the hope that from even the most difficult circumstances good will result and it is from this hope that faith grows.

Love Endures All Things

No matter how difficult, no matter how many problems and trials face us, there is only one thing that can endure all the attacks. Were it not for the love of Christ we share with one another, Satan would long ago have had his way, broken us down, placed us under his thumb, and led us to death. Paul was beaten and left for dead, imprisoned, shipwrecked, bitten by a snake, and afflicted by a "thorn in the flesh" in his service to the gospel. Yet he could still write with conviction:

For I am sure that neither death, nor life, nor angels,

nor principalities, nor things present, nor things to come, nor powers, nor height, nor depth, nor anything else in all creation, will be able to separate us from the love of God in Christ Jesus our Lord. (Rom. 8:38-39)

By sharing Christ's love with others we share the strength to endure all things. If we fail to share we leave others weak and open to attack from the evil one. Every time we act in an unloving way we aid the work of the devil. Every time we react to a situation with love we increase another's resistance to evil and help to bring Satan closer to his final punishment!

Love Never Fails
Eternal God is love. Therefore, love is eternal, never-ending. This world will come to an end, but love will continue on into eternity. Love is the eternal bond between the saints on earth and in heaven. Love has always existed and always will exist. To plant a seed of love is to plant an eternal seed that will grow and bear fruit for eternity.

This brief meditation is only an introduction to the internal attitude we call love, specifically the Christ-love we all desire to live in. While love will always be expressed in external acts, it is truly an attitude of the heart that highly esteems others and seeks only their good. As managers we must feel free to apply this gift of love to all we work with, in every situation, always seeking to achieve good for the other.

Practicing Love Toward Your Staff
We have been discussing how to practice love in our

relationships with our employees. The following are some more practical suggestions on how managers can be loving at work. Many of the ideas presented below are adapted from an excellent little book by Morton T. Kelsey, *The Art of Christian Love*,[4] which is recommended reading for all who want to better understand how to love others as they should.

1. Be a cheerful servant to all you work with, including your staff. Do not hesitate to give yourself for them.
2. Consider no one superior to another but learn to recognize the limitations and special gifts that each has and the contribution each makes to the work group.
3. Provide an example of love to your staff. Do not simply speak love, but act it in a tangible way. Let love permeate your every action and decision.
4. Do not boast of your accomplishments but recognize the contributions of others that make your work possible.
5. Teach your staff how to live the Christian life and be open to learn from any source, including those under your authority.
6. Exercise authority in a just and loving manner, always considering the impact a decision will have on those who work for you.
7. Seek to improve the status of your fellow-man even at your own expense. Learn to willingly sacrifice yourself for the sake of others.
8. Always stand for the truth, never put it aside to make things easier.
9. Forgive the faults and mistakes of others and help them improve.
10. Discipline lovingly and consistently rather than by ignoring wrongdoing.

[4]Morton T. Kelsey, *The Art Of Christian Love* (Dove Publications: Pecos, N.M., 1974), pp. 31-33.

11. Encourage your staff and reward them for good work.
12. Above all, be open to the Lord and seek His guidance in your daily work relationships and decisions. Submit yourself totally to Him and expect light from Him to make your path straight. Allow the Spirit of God to work freely in you, using you in service to those sent to you.

12

The Responsibility
of the Manager

When they had finished breakfast, Jesus said to
Simon Peter, "Simon, son of John, do you love me
more than these?" He said to him, "Yes, Lord; you
know that I love you." He said to him, "Feed my
lambs." A second time he said to him, "Simon, son of
John, do you love me?" He said to him, "Yes, Lord;
you know that I love you." He said to him, "Tend my
sheep." He said to him the third time, "Simon, son of
John, do you love me?" Peter was grieved because he
said to him the third time, "Do you love me?" And he
said to him, "Lord, you know everything; you know
that I love you." Jesus said to him, "Feed my sheep."
(John 21:15-17)

All who are called to a pastoral ministry have received
the commission to care for the flock of Christ. When Jesus
said, "Feed my lambs"; "Tend my sheep"; and "Feed my
sheep," He outlined the responsibility of those He
appoints as pastors. As managers, it is our responsibility
to carry out this commission as part of our daily work.

Carried Out in Love

The commission is three-fold with each part given following Jesus' request for a confession of love on the part of Peter. Much has been written on this passage but here it is important for us to focus on the necessity for Peter to confess his love for Jesus, before the Lord assigned the pastoral responsibility to him. Before we can minister to the needs of others we must make a loving commitment to Christ, for in loving Him we find the love we need to minister to His body, His people. The primary requirement of those called to the pastoral ministry is the same for each Christian. That is, "You shall love the Lord your God with all your heart, and with all your soul, and with all your mind" (Matt. 22:37). Then you will be able to "love your neighbor as yourself" (Matt. 22:39).

A Word on Priority

We have already considered the heterogeneity of the manager's staff. Because it will generally be a mix of Christians and non-Christians, a question arises regarding our priorities in work and ministry. By being first a manager and then a minister, *all* employees must be treated equally in the performance of the management portion of the job. However, when we move into the realm of ministry, a definite priority must be established if the manager is to be able to blend the diverse elements of management and ministry.

The Galatians seemed to have faced similar situations and the apostle advised them, "So then, as we have opportunity, let us do good to all men, and especially to those who are of the household of faith" (Gal. 6:10). By the use of the word "especially" a priority is established. The "household of faith" is the body of Christ. The body of

Christ is not limited to Catholics, Baptists, Lutherans, or whatever denomination you belong to. It is, rather, the grouping of all who profess Christ as Lord and Savior. Therefore, in ministry, the manager is to give priority to carrying out Christ's commission by caring for his brothers and sisters in the Lord.

While other Christians have the priority on our time for ministry, this does not mean we are to exclude non-Christians. We are to love all men and "do good to all men" as time permits and the opportunity presents itself. The methods will differ as will the type of ministry but the manager does have a ministerial responsibility to nonbelievers as well. What is important is for the manager to remember the priority that has been established and then to minister as the Spirit of God leads.

Feeding the Lambs

The lambs are the young, new members of the flock. They are the weakest and the most in need of care. The shepherd must spend much time and effort tending to the lambs of the flock and seeing that they are nourished so that they can grow into strong and healthy sheep. Because of their youth and weakness the shepherd must do much more for them than for the larger of his flock. The shepherd's responsibility to the lambs also includes being present and assisting at the birth of new members of the flock, helping them in those first months of weakness, welcoming them as they come into their place in the flock, and insuring that they are properly fed. Thus, the shepherd sees that the lambs are cared for and that they receive the nourishment they must have as they begin their new life.

At the office this involves sharing with others what

Jesus has done and is continuing to do in your life. It means using the Word of God in counseling, decision making, or whenever it is appropriate to refer to its authority. Most importantly, this witness includes living a life that reflects the presence of the Holy Spirit. It is letting the light of Christ shine in you and radiate from you at all times.

At the same time the manager must be cautious not to blind others with this light or to badger them about spiritual matters when they are not interested. Such an infringement on another is spiritual nagging and can be destructive, tearing down whatever good has already been done. The manager must be sensitive to the other's receptiveness and should never pursue spiritual matters when he senses any reluctance on the part of the other. The manager must approach this portion of his ministry with much sensitivity, discernment, gentleness, and most importantly, patience.

When you are walking in the Spirit and conscious of your commission almost any situation can be an opportunity to bring in Christ without forcing it. Learn to tune your spirit to the things of God, to practice His presence constantly and make Him a part of your every moment. Do not let the fear of scoffing or unreceptiveness keep you from forever proclaiming the glory of God and His only Son. Let everyone know where you stand spiritually. If Christ is at the center of your life let Him be at the center of your conversations, meetings, decisions and actions. Jesus is interested in everything you do and if you will let Him, He will help you in all situations. And the best way to let Him is to acknowledge His part in everything you do. We should constantly pray, "Hear, O Lord, and be gracious to me! O Lord, be thou my helper!"

(Ps. 30:10), and "Let the words of my mouth and the meditation of my heart be acceptable in thy sight, O Lord, my rock and my redeemer" (Ps. 19:14).

In taking this attitude toward my commission I have been led to allow the Holy Spirit to work freely in my office and in all I do. This has resulted in interviews and counseling sessions in which much of the time is spent witnessing about Christ when others are receptive and the ministry fits into the framework of the session. At meetings I freely refer to the Scripture for guidance and help in solving problems and making decisions.

Some of this sharing of the Lord is evangelistic, bringing the gospel message to the attention of the non-Christians I work with. However, there is also the opportunity to teach and share the basic truths of the Christian faith with some of the less mature Christians on my staff. One secretary knew the Lord for several years but had not truly given her entire life over to Him. She had not yet claimed the victory of Christ. When faced with serious family and financial problems she came to know Jesus as a person and found the strength to live a victorious, joyful life. After this, she shared with me that the example and teaching of strong Christians in the office had brought her to this realization which had transformed her life.

All of this is not a waste of the employer's time. When Jesus is placed first, sharing and teaching comes about as a natural part of the conduct of business and is beneficial to the organization. Even those times that are primarily counseling are a legitimate part of the manager's job if not one of the most important. Unless the employee is at peace, whether physically, psychologically, emotionally, or spiritually, he or she will not be the best producer at work. Thus, the manager's counseling efforts should be designed to help the employees resolve whatever problems they have.

Aside from the primarily spiritual realm, the manager feeds the lambs in still other ways. This generally includes orientating and training new employees. The manager cares for them by showing them what is expected and helping them to get to know the others they will be working with.

All of this is designed to bring the employees to the point where they require less direct attention, strengthening them as they grow in maturity. Once they mature they require less constant care, but they still must be tended to and fed. It is to these responsibilities we next turn.

Tending the Sheep

Even when the lambs become full-grown sheep they require care. Though they are very independent, there are many things sheep cannot do for themselves and the shepherd tends to these needs. The shepherd protects the flock from danger, he provides security for them so that they can graze and grow in peace. He tends to their injuries and cares for them in sickness. The shepherd also leads the sheep about, keeping them on a safe path, and if they wander, he sets out to rescue them.

An important part of the manager's responsibility is to listen to his staff. He must be available to them and disposed to listen as they share their problems, ideas, needs, joys and sorrows with him. By listening carefully he can learn about the specific needs of his staff and tend to them before they become problems. Listening leads often to prayer about the things that are detected when we really hear the other person. Prayer for his staff is one of the primary means the manager uses to tend to his sheep. Through prayer we can express our total dependence on the Father and bring our needs to Him. Only when supported by an undergirding of prayer can the manager stand against those who would attack and harm the flock.

An important part of this care for the flock includes correcting those who go astray and by this correction or discipline rescuing them from the hand of Satan. Correction must be made according to the model given us by God and will be discussed in greater detail in a later chapter. In essence we are to do as Paul instructed Timothy:

> And the Lord's servant must not be quarrelsome but kindly to every one, an apt teacher, forbearing, correcting his opponents with gentleness. God may perhaps grant that they will repent and come to know the truth, and they may escape from the snare of the devil, after being captured by him to do his will. (2 Tim. 2:24-26)

False teaching abounds and it is easy for a person to be led astray without understanding what is happening. Newspapers all carry horoscopes; mind-control techniques like transcendental meditation, are being tailored to the mass market; popular television programs build shows around the occult and witchcraft; and many false religions like the Worldwide Church of God are playing to the spiritual hunger of the populace. All of these things are dangerous, opening the participant to the influence of Satan and his forces. The manager must be especially on the watch for his Christian employees that they do not stray into danger. If they do he must pray for them, correct them, and gently do all that he can to bring them back to the flock.

A manager also ministers to his employees by providing them with an example of a dedicated disciple of Christ. By his attitude, approach to difficulties and overall disposition the manager can either present a good picture of a Christian that stimulates others to walk closer to Christ; or he can present a picture that turns others away from the Lord.

Other daily needs he must tend to include encouragement when times are difficult; counsel and guidance to help the employee grow; the explanation of what the Word teaches on a subject that is important to the person, like child-rearing or divorce; or recognition of something the person has done that is evidence of growth.

Aside from the spiritual, the manager tends to his staff by providing guidance on how to improve work, interpretation and promulgation of policies and procedures that make it easier for the employee to understand what is expected of him and how to accomplish it. Counsel about personal problems or difficulties one is having at work is also an important part of this care.

Daily care, no matter how insignificant it may appear, is necessary for the employees. If they do not receive it from the Christian manager they may seek it from a less truthful source. They may feel rejected and hide within themselves, or become so dissatisfied that a negative attitude begins to permeate the work situation. Unless they are cared for, they live in danger and will not continue to grow and mature but will be subject to the ravages of the world and Satan. As Christ tends to all of us as His flock, He expects us to tend to the flocks He has assigned to us.

Feeding the Sheep

Feeding is part of the tending and care of the sheep. Proper feeding is the means by which the shepherd insures they receive the nourishment they need to continue living a healthy life. This continued feeding is so important that our Lord emphasized it by making it an additional charge to the tending of the flock.

Lambs are fed first on the milk of their mothers. A soft and easily digestible food is necessary because their young stomachs are not yet capable of handling more solid foods that are difficult to digest. To draw an analogy, spiritual lambs are fed spiritual milk, the basic and most necessary truths of Christianity. These include man's sinfulness, his need for a Savior, the atoning death of Christ, and man's salvation through the acceptance of Jesus as Lord and Savior.

As the young Christian grows, he must have more solid spiritual food to nourish him. If he receives only the basics he will not grow strong and will soon become bored or will develop a misconception of what it means to live as a Christian. Instead, he needs to be fed the solid food that deals with the life of discipleship, spiritual warfare, ministry, living a victorious life, spiritual authority and other such topics. Paul writes, "For every one who lives on milk is unskilled in the word of righteousness, for he is a child. But solid food is for the mature, for those who have their faculties trained by practice to distinguish good from evil" (Heb. 5:13-14).

Let me share an example. Not long ago, I began to share some of my spiritual experiences with an engineer who works on my staff. He had accepted Christ as his Savior when he was a child but, by his own admission, was not walking very close to the Master despite his efforts to live a good life. Morally, he was unmarred by the gross sinfulness so many of us fall prey to when we are not walking in the power of Christ. After several talks he told me he wanted to get closer to the Lord. I began to pray for him and share with him about the change that had occurred in my life when I had been baptized in the Holy Spirit. He had never heard about this powerful Christian life that is possible when you are overflowing with the Spirit and he was hungry for it. He was fed with the Scriptures, several good books, and a living Christian witness. Not long after this began he was certain he needed to give himself totally to the Lord and sought the baptism in the Spirit. He received it and is now living as a shining witness to the Lord.

There are many ways in which the manager can prepare and serve this spiritual food to his staff at work. Individual sharing and the giving of good teaching books, like I did with the engineer, is one way. Another that has been successful in my office has been the establishment of a lunch hour Bible study. I have several Christians on my staff and there are many others in the department. The Lord showed me that many of these Christians were longing for solid food. The result was a Bible study that lasted for several months before the Lord led us to other commitments. This group, at which at least seven different denominations were represented, freely shared what the Scriptures meant to them. Everyone had an opportunity to share, to learn from others, and grow in strength.

Feeding the sheep applies to all areas of our lives. As

employees grow in their jobs and become competent, there is often a tendency for them to become less than enthusiastic about their work. It is the manager's responsibility to help employees continue to grow by assigning new and challenging tasks or by giving them new responsibilities.

Reassignment renews interest at the same time as helping them to grow in skill and competence. It further benefits the organization by making happier and better producing employees who are more versatile and more valuable to the organization.

As we have seen, care and feeding of the sheep are the primary responsibilities of the pastoral minister. It is essential that the manager provide this care if he is to accept and carry out the ministry that is a part of his job. But what if he chooses not to?

Failure to Do Your Job

The manager is not forced into ministry. He is free to accept or reject the commission to the pastoral ministry. He must decide whether or not to accept the spiritual responsibility which is inherent in the nature of management.

When deciding whether we will accept the commission we should not all expect to be equally capable ministers. We need to recognize that not all managers will be as experienced and gifted as others in spiritual matters, but we also need to understand that the Lord knows this and does not measure us one against another. He knows what we can handle and what is in our hearts to motivate us. He asks that we do the best we can and make a sincere effort to care for the flock He has placed in our charge. He understands our limitations and does not punish us for them. The only true failure we can have is to disobey the Lord's command to serve our employees through love. God's Word has a strong warning to give to those who would shun their responsibility.

"Woe to the shepherds who destroy and scatter the sheep of my pasture!" says the Lord. Therefore thus says the Lord, the God of Israel, concerning the shepherds who care for my people: "You have scattered my flock, and have driven them away, and you have not attended to them. Behold, I will attend to you for your evil doings, says the Lord. Then I will gather the remnant of my flock out of all the countries where I have driven them, and I will bring them back to their fold, and they shall be fruitful and multiply. I will set shepherds over them who will care for them, and they shall fear no more, nor be dismayed, neither shall any be missing, says the Lord." (Jer. 23:1-4)

The word of the Lord came to me: "Son of man, prophesy against the shepherds of Israel, prophesy and say to them, even to the shepherds, Thus says the Lord God: Ho, shepherds of Israel who have been feeding yourselves! Should not shepherds feed the sheep?" (Ezek. 34:1-2)

The lessons here are clear. We have certain responsibilities that require us to care for and serve the flock we have been assigned. If we fail to do it we will have to answer to the Lord. The above quoted prophecies exemplify the place God has assigned to the pastoral ministry. This is something all who are called to tend the flock must carefully consider as they go about their work.

13

Communications in Christian Management

I tell you, on the day of judgment men will render account for every careless word they utter; for by your words you will be justified, and by your words you will be condemned. (Matt. 12:36-37)

Communication is an important building block of good relationships. Effective, proper communication fosters understanding of one another and brings us closer together. Management is people-oriented, therefore one of the most critical tasks of the manager is that of communication. Manager and staff must have open lines of communication in order to direct, correct, instruct, clarify and encourage. Furthermore, good communication must characterize not only the manager-staff relationship, but the staff-staff and staff-client relationships as well. A proverb illustrates the importance of this, "An unreliable messenger can cause a lot of trouble. Reliable communication permits progress" (Prov. 13:17 TLB).

Nearly every management book written today includes a chapter or at least a section on communications. Courses on how to communicate more effectively are offered by universities, at private companies and government agencies. All of this serves to emphasize the significance that being able to communicate has in management. Management author, O. Jeff Harris, Jr., sums up this emphasis as follows:

> Communication is the exchange of ideas or concepts for purposes of information, command and instruction, influences and persuasion, or integration. Without some type of communication, no organization will exist long. Without accurate, meaningful communication, no organization will be successful. Managers bear a heavy responsibility for the creation of a proper environment for communication and for establishing and maintaining the necessary organizational communication channels. Senders and receivers both bear a responsibility for the successful interpretation and understanding of messages communicated. Communication barriers exist in abundance, but most of the problems they present can be overcome with proper attention and effort.[1]

This chapter will seek to help the Christian manager to establish a perspective from which he can begin to give the proper attention to the communications network in his organization.

A Scriptural Perspective
The present author suggests that the manager consult and carefully study some of the excellent material that is now available on effective management communication.

[1] O. Jeff Harris, Jr., *Managing People At Work: Concepts and Cases In Interpersonal Behavior* (John Wiley & Sons, Inc.: New York, 1976), pp. 264-265.

Much research and scholarship has been devoted to this important area and the manager can benefit from this. For this reason the present chapter will not attempt to cover the subject from the same perspective. However, since communication is critical to all phases of management and is essential to every relationship, this chapter will present a scriptural perspective of the topic.

Words

Words, whether spoken or written, are our primary tools of communication. We use words to express how we feel, give meaning to our thoughts, to seek solutions to problems. The whole of our thinking, reasoning and communicating process uses words. The Bible abounds in instruction on the proper use of the tongue which, in a modern world that places great emphasis on the written word, apply equally well to that mode of communication. Each manager must be conscious of implications of the improper use of words and ways to guard against the danger.

Jesus used words to teach about the kingdom of God. He knew that words which come out of our mouths are formed by the feelings and thoughts within us. He was attacked with words and condemmed to death with them. Yet, He also knows that words can be used to comfort others, to express love and compassion, to teach, to encourage and to praise God. The way words are used by any person, He taught, is guided according to what is in the person's heart. If malice and hatred dwell inside a person, the same will roll off the tongue. If wisdom, love and gentleness fill a person, the same will compose his speech. Jesus said:

"Hear and understand: not what goes into the mouth defiles a man, but what comes out of the mouth, this defiles a man. . . . Do you not see that whatever goes into the mouth passes into the stomach, and so passes on? But what comes out of the mouth proceeds from the heart, and this defiles a man. For out of the heart come evil thoughts, murder, adultery, fornication, theft, false witness, slander. These are what defile a man; but to eat with unwashed hands does not defile a man." (Matt. 15:10-11, 17-20)

In reflection on this teaching, the Holy Spirit speaks through James:

So the tongue is a little member and boasts of great things. How great a forest is set ablaze by a small fire!
And the tongue is a fire. The tongue is an unrighteous world among our members, staining the whole body, setting on fire the cycle of nature, and set on fire by hell. For every kind of beast and bird, of reptile and sea creature, can be tamed and has been tamed by humankind, but no human being can tame the tongue—a restless evil, full of deadly poison. With it we bless the Lord and Father, and with it we curse men, who are made in the likeness of God. From the same mouth come blessing and cursing. My brethren, this ought not to be so. Does a spring pour forth from the same opening fresh water and brackish? Can a fig tree, my brethren, yield olives, or a grapevine figs? No more can salt water yield fresh. (James 3:5-12)

If the tongue is so dangerous and cannot be tamed, have

we any hope of civil communication? Or will our relationships be plagued with the hurts inflicted by the improper use of words? Left to ourselves our tongues will remain uncontrolled. But if we submit our use of words to Jesus as we are to submit every portion of our lives, the door will be opened for the Holy Spirit to gain the control we lack.

Two-Way Communication

When we regularly watch the television news we can become accustomed to hearing a certain reporter and grow partial to his or her style to the point that we are not comfortable with other reporters. This communication is essentially one-way. The newscaster speaks and we listen. Except for an infrequent letter expressing our opinion on a matter, there is no back and forth exchange of words, ideas or thoughts. Therefore, however we might enjoy hearing that reporter, we do not have a personal relationship with the individual.

Personal relationships, in particular that of manager and staff, require that communication be two-way. This may appear to be self-evident but serious management problems too often occur because we fail to make communication with our staff reciprocal in nature. Unless we can both hear and respond to the other and the other can both hear and respond to us, we are not really communicating. All parties must be both speakers and listeners. The wisdom of the Bible says there is "a time to keep silence, and a time to speak" (Eccles. 3:7). The manager cannot only give direction, he must also be able to hear what his staff would say to him.

A busy manager often finds himself faced with deadlines and pressured to keep up with even routine matters. As a result, many managers have the tendency to seek the quickest way to a decision. What is most unfortunate here is the likelihood that the manager will seek to speed things up by not taking the time to communicate with others who are involved. Even if he asks for input he may not really hear what is being said because his mind is preoccupied with other matters; or he might not take adequate time to hear all of what he should and then make a decision based on incomplete information. Probably one of the most common and most costly problems in money, morale, time and other resources is the manager's failure to listen to his staff.

An employee cannot be properly directed, instructed, corrected or acknowledged unless the manager learns to listen. If we do not hear what the other person is trying to communicate to us, our responses will be incomplete, inadequate and too frequently wrong. If we fail to listen to the other, we will base our communication only on our opinions and perceptions which are themselves subject to distortion and error. The penalty for failing to listen is inefficiency, ineffectiveness, increased cost, waste and the creation of more problems and difficulties of increasing seriousness.

Two-way communication provides needed direction for both the manager and staff. A shepherd may lead his flock into the pasture by calling them but unless he hears the bleating of the lamb who has fallen into a pit he cannot rescue it. The lesson for the manager is: *Speak, listen and act only after you have considered what you have heard.* This builds trust and closeness in the relationship. Consider everything said to you by a staff member to be worthy of acknowledgment and investigation. This does not mean to accept everything at face value but to realize it would not be said without a reason. Search out the reason and take the action that is necessary. An employee who is always making suggestions on improving work processes may be telling you that he has other skills or that his job is not challenging enough. Understanding this can help you to better utilize this employee, making his job better for him and more valuable for the organization.

A Trust Builder

An attitude of trust on the part of the staff toward the manager and by the manager for the staff is an essential element in the building of a good working environment. Good communications help to establish this trust.

Often it is an absence of information or a misunderstanding of what was said that causes a lack of trust. God's revelation to us is an example of good communication. His Word clearly outlines His plan for us. It specifies what is expected of us and clearly presents His promises. When we read the Bible there is no doubt as to what our choices are: life or death. Our Father has given us His Word in order that we have a clear conception of whom we are being asked to trust in. Jesus' life on earth was part of this continuing effort of God to reveal himself to us. It is through this ultimate revelation of God becoming man that God seeks to help us understand Him. He wants us to have no misconception or to have any lack of information that would hinder our faith.

In management, our communications must be as complete, careful and clear as the essential message of God's salvation. All management communication, regardless of the source and receiver, must possess these qualities. It must be complete in presenting all the necessary information to make the transmission understandable and truthful. Nothing should be omitted or added that would cause its meaning to be altered from what is true. "Put away from you crooked speech, and put devious talk far from you" (Prov. 4:24).

It must be presented in a careful manner. Words said in anger seldom are heard beyond the receiver's perception of the anger. Also, hurried or otherwise sloppily prepared and/or delivered messages often add to confusion and contribute to misunderstanding. Words are less liable to misunderstanding and are better received when the communicator takes the time to carefully present the message. "The wise of heart is called a man of discernment, and pleasant speech increases persuasiveness" (Prov. 16:21).

Trust is established through reliable communications. Scripture tells us that good words have a healthful effect on the whole person. "There is one whose rash words are like sword thrusts, but the tongue of the wise brings healing" (Prov. 12:18) and, "Pleasant words are like a honeycomb, sweetness to the soul and health to the body" (Prov. 16:24). Wherever trust abounds we will find sound relationships between healthy people (in body, mind and spirit).

Common Errors in Communication

It is doubtful that there has been one person, with the exception of Jesus Christ, who never got into trouble or caused harm by the improper use of words. Family squabbles, arguments at work, disagreements and misunderstandings with the neighbors, are all often the result of a stinging word flung off a hasty tongue. Proverbs says, "He who keeps his mouth and his tongue keeps himself out of trouble" (Prov. 21:23).

Before we can begin to correct a problem, it must be identified. Therefore, let us briefly consider some of the common errors we make in our communicating.

1. *Speaking without thinking*—We often respond to another with the first words that come to our lips. When we do this we usually have not taken the time to weigh our response and can easily bring forth something we really do not mean. This is especially dangerous because the person who is expecting our response will tend to latch on to the initial words and any further explanation may be disregarded altogether, or add confusion and doubt—all of which render the communication ineffective.

2. *Jumping to conclusions*—When we lack the patience to gather all the facts we can about a given situation we base our communications on incomplete information. Thus, we may be told of a staff member's infraction of policy from another individual and decide on disciplinary action before studying the policy and hearing the viewpoints of the others involved, including the accused individual.

3. *Passing rumors*—For some reason people seem to enjoy sharing every tidbit of information they have access to, however incomplete, inconsequential or erroneous. This causes rumors which grow in magnitude as they spread from person to person. Rumors are also common when people try to guess what is missing from a communication. In any case, rumors have the devastating effect of causing many of the hearers to believe and act on something that is patently false. Any manager can understand the serious implications of this.

4. *Pronouncing judgment*—Despite all of God's warnings in the Bible we persist in our judging of others for what they have done or failed to do. This, and its

companion fault of *slandering* others, detract from the true purpose of communication which is to build good, healthy relationships. It prevents this not only between the judge and the person being judged but also between those who hear the judge's pronouncement and the one being judged by creating a false and not too desirable image of the person.

5. *Failure to listen*—We have already mentioned this but it needs to be reemphasized that a common fault is our ability to tune others out so that we respond without listening or do not respond at all when a response is expected.

Every problem and error in communication results from man's sinfulness which has made him subject to the whims and fancies of the world, his own flesh, and the deceptions of Satan. By His redeeming death and resurrection, Jesus makes it possible for us, through this grace, to overcome these deficiencies.

Overcoming Communication Problems

While it is in Christ and by His Spirit that it is possible for us to redeem our use of words and transform it into a gift bringing glory to God, the transformation does not occur unless we are willing to participate and work according to the Spirit's leading to overcome these problems. The following, then, are some rules that will help us to improve our ability to communicate with each other.

Think before speaking. "Do you see a man who is hasty in his words? There is more hope for a fool than for him" (Prov. 29:20). Even a fool is wiser than the man who speaks without thinking. We should all cultivate the habit of knowing what we are going to say before we open our mouths. This means we should weigh and evaluate the effect our words will have on the hearer. If it is something of a serious nature, such as in giving a correction, take a moment to check with the Holy Spirit to see if what you are planning to say is proper. Ask yourself, "Would I say this to Jesus?" Remember, "The mind of the righteous ponders how to answer, but the mouth of the wicked pours out evil things" (Prov. 15:28).

Listen first. "If one gives answer before he hears, it is his folly and shame" (Prov. 18:13). There is much danger inherent in speaking in response to someone without first hearing what is said. To hear means more than to simply listen to what is said. It means to actually hear, consider, think about and reflect on the meaning of the statement. Real hearing is not the perception of sounds but the grasping of the meaning of what is conveyed. Therefore, when we exhort to listen first we mean to pay attention to all the details of the communication, particularly the words, the way they are pronounced or stressed, and the mannerisms of the speaker that add meaning to the words. All of this helps to convey the message. We must learn to hear with our eyes, ears and mind before we respond.

Say only good. "Let no evil talk come out of your mouths, but only such as is good for edifying, as fits the occasion, that it may impart grace to those who hear" (Eph. 4:29). We should never say anything that will slander another or hurt them in any way. Whatever we say, be it encouragement, instruction or correction, it must be done in such a way that it helps the other person grow. It must be edifying rather than deflating. Grace is something given us by God. The way that the concept is used in the above quotation implies that our communications must be such that they bring something of God's very own goodness to those we are in contact with. Therefore, there is no place for insult or any other form of injurious remark.

Never speak in anger. "The vexation of a fool is known at once, but the prudent man ignores an insult" (Prov. 12:16). It is dangerous to open our mouths or write a memo when we are angry and upset about something. It is much wiser to wait until the initial heat has passed before speaking or responding. At times, when I am upset over some policy or decision I disagree with, I will hastily write a stinging memorandum to my superior. Then, I put the memo in my desk for several days before finalizing it. Usually I decide not to send it at all, or, if I do forward it, I change it substantially to take the acid out of it. I know that this practice has saved me from much embarrassment, kept me from harming others, and probably has kept me from losing my job. We all need to learn that angry words cause the initial problem to become more serious than it really is.

Never speak unnecessarily. "When words are many, transgression is not lacking, but he who restrains his lips is prudent" (Prov. 10:19). When we talk too much we do not have time to think about what we are saying and we add confusion rather than clarity. Since unnecessary talk is usually foolish or silly it causes the listener to tune out and not hear what is said, even if it is of importance. Talk too much as a habit and you will never be heard. The wise manager chooses words that communicate, that get the message across without any unnecessary or irrelevant baggage.

Speak only truth. "A false witness will not go unpunished, and he who utters lies will not escape" (Prov. 19:5). To state it bluntly, there is never any excuse for the

Christian to lie. Nothing justifies falsehood; deceit is always a sin. When a manager cannot share information with his staff he should not lie because of it. If this is the case he should be honest with the inquirer and tell him that the matter is confidential.

Remember that words set the mood. "A soft answer turns away wrath, but a harsh word stirs up anger" (Prov. 15:1). "A word fitly spoken is like apples of gold in a setting of silver" (Prov. 25:11). The words used in a letter or conversation will help set the mood of the reader or listener. Angry, critical words will cause communication to be guarded, tense and angry in response. Kind, gentle, loving words will create an atmosphere of peace and cooperation that will allow open and profitable communication.

Learning to Communicate

Learning to communicate properly is a lifelong task. We will often make mistakes but as we become more sensitive to others and more aware of how we affect them, the errors will become fewer. Skill in communication is especially critical to the success of the manager-staff relationship. The proper use of words can build trust and help establish good working conditions. Improper communication can be devastating. Rumors, angry words and the like can tear down trust and build barriers, all to the detriment of the organization and rendering the manager ineffective in his work and ministry.

We must commit ourselves to following the guidance of the Holy Spirit and earnestly seek to learn to use words in a way that is pleasing to God. To this end we should pray with David, "Set a guard over my mouth, O Lord, keep watch over the door of my lips!" (Ps. 141:3).

14

A Christian Perspective on Some Key Managerial Functions

And the Lord's servant must not be quarrelsome but kindly to every one, an apt teacher, forbearing, correcting his opponents with gentleness. (2 Tim. 2:24-25)

A manager and his staff are constantly interacting. Because he is dealing with people whose lives are affected by their jobs, the manager must spend a significant amount of time in working with employees on a one-to-one basis. This contact often involves counseling and guidance, discipline and reward, teaching and instruction or some combination of these sorts of interaction.

Obviously the manager cannot be expected to also be a professional psychologist and certified teacher at the same time. Yet, the proper handling of staff in these critical situations is important to the performance of the job. A manager must learn to cultivate the skills needed to help people in what are frequently difficult and potentially explosive situations.

This is no easy task but he must be comfortable and competent when working with his staff in any situation they may face. This means he must develop a sensitivity that will allow him to recognize a person's needs and he must be able to help meet these needs. Specialized training and experience in these areas is a valuable help but, by themselves, these are insufficient. To be a successful counselor, disciplinarian or teacher, the manager must supplement technical expertise with reliance on God. The Lord wants us to be aware of, and know how to use, the knowledge we have available about interacting with others. He also wants us to use it according to His will which is that we approach the individuals we are working with in love and with gentleness. The methods and techniques we use are, in the Christian perspective, tools to be used as the Lord directs, for the good of the person we are ministering to.

In this chapter we will briefly examine and comment on what the Scriptures say about the manager's responsibility regarding these three key managerial functions.

Discipline and Reward

It is the manager's job to control and direct the operations of the work place, to coordinate the efforts of the staff in order to perform tasks assigned, and to achieve the objectives that have been set. To accomplish this, the manager must maintain a certain level of discipline which requires obedience to established rules, policies and procedures. To achieve the required performance it is necessary to establish and maintain discipline. When an employee does his work well he should be rewarded to encourage him and others to continue to perform well. On the other hand, if an employee does poorly or breaks the rules, he must be corrected and disciplinary action must be taken. It is the responsibility of the manager to both give rewards and discipline.

"A liberal man will be enriched, and one who waters will himself be watered" (Prov. 11:25). The recognition of good work will bring forth more good work. Excellent and exceptional performance should be rewarded with salary increases, bonuses and promotions; but perhaps the most important reward is a word of acknowledgment and thanks given an employee for doing his job well. Most employees are average, rather than exceptional, performers but their consistent and loyal efforts form a solid core of production around which the organization builds. These efforts are too often ignored and must be recognized.

Try telling your secretary that you appreciate her usual neat typing as well as giving her time off for spending extra hours on a special assignment. Commend the lathe operator for his lack of waste as well as giving him a bonus for above-average production. Such reward is a recognition of each individual's value to the organization and to the manager. It is a way of saying, "You are important to me and the company; we appreciate you." This reward helps to improve the person's self-esteem, making him or her happier and more eager to be a part of the team, knowing they are accepted and needed.

We all like to do things that make others feel good so the giving of rewards is not a difficult task. Equally important, but much more difficult to do, is to discipline an employee. Since this is not a pleasant task, managers can easily go to either of two extremes when faced with situations requiring discipline. They may shy away from and not carry out necessary discipline, or they may prepare themselves for the task by working up a false attitude of anger toward the employee.

Both of these extremes can be avoided if we recognize that to discipline someone is an act of love and must be done in a loving way. "My son, do not regard lightly the discipline of the Lord, nor lose courage when you are punished by him. For the Lord disciplines him whom he loves, and chastises every son whom he receives" (Heb. 12:5-6).

Our Father loves us and corrects us so that we will be better children, living a more pleasant and fulfilled life. This is the reason we discipline our employees. Discipline, done in love, is a way to a better life, a positive means of growth. Though it does not always seem so, the results are beneficial. "For the moment all discipline seems painful rather than pleasant; later it yields the peaceful fruit of righteousness to those who have been trained by it" (Heb. 12:11). Praise God for His loving discipline of His children!

By taking the time to correct an employee you are indicating your interest in his or her well-being. We fail to correct when we lack love and are unconcerned about allowing another to continue in error without direction.

Discipline must be gentle to be effective. Done in anger it is as useless as no discipline at all. Rather than focusing on the corrective part of the process, the employee will focus on the hostility of the manager. Nothing will impress him but this hostility and his own reaction to it. Thus the disciplinary action will not improve or correct the situation.

The proper use of reward and punishment includes their fair application. The reward or punishment must be commensurate with the work or transgression; it must be deserved. Someone should not receive a major promotion for accomplishing routine assignments nor should he be demoted for reporting late once or twice. The capricious exercise of authority will eventually render the manager ineffective by destroying the staff's perception of him. God treats us justly and demands that we treat our employees the same. To paraphrase Scripture, "[Managers], treat your [employees] justly and fairly, knowing that you also have a [Manager] in heaven" (Col. 4:1).

In applying rewards and punishments the manager must remember that his job is to evaluate, measure and judge the work of the employee, not the person himself. To be a personal judge is to violate the clear commandment of Christ (Matt. 7:1-5). However, the manager does have a legitimate responsibility to evaluate the work of his staff. Just as a father has the obligation to make judgments about family matters, the manager has the duty to maintain order in his staff in the same fashion so long as he does not attempt to apply his authority beyond the requirements of the employee's job.

Discipline will be ineffective if we fail to forgive the mistakes of our employees. When we fail to forgive we are being prideful and selfishly placing our own feelings and desires ahead of the other person. Rather than bearing grudges and keeping count of their mistakes, forgive them, "For if you forgive men their trespasses, your heavenly Father also will forgive you; but if you do not forgive men their trespasses, neither will your Father forgive your trespasses" (Matt. 6:14).

Our conscience tells us when we have done wrong and when we have harmed another we want to make amends. If the person we have wronged does not forgive us we experience a painful blow by the unloving action. Failure to forgive an employee binds that person to their guilt and indicates that you do not care for them. This can lead to serious problems in the relationship, not the least of which is continued disregard for authority by the employee. Strained relations can be relieved by the act of forgiveness.

The manager is often placed in a position requiring him to correct or reward a staff member. In all cases he must ask the Holy Spirit to guide him in the action. He must strive for gentleness and fairness. Furthermore, the manager should always act in love and be ready to apply the healing balm of forgiveness to any difficult situation.

Counseling and Guidance

The manager must be able and willing to direct and guide his staff in their work. When an employee is faced with a problem that is affecting his or her work, the manager is often required to become a counselor. For example, it is usually essential to counsel with the person who is frequently absent. It is through such required counseling that more serious needs that are deeply imbedded in an individual's personal life are brought to the surface. Frequent absences, to develop the example, may be a symptom of a serious drinking problem or strained relations with a spouse. While the manager cannot and should not force someone into a counseling session about a matter that is revealed in such a fashion, the growing closeness of the manager-staff relationship may cause the person to seek his supervisor's advice. The more sensitive and available the manager is, the more likely he will be called upon to act as a counselor to staff who find themselves with problems that may not directly relate to the job.

No problem is ever completely divorced from the work place and it would be harmful to the individual and to the others at work to ignore a request for help. Problems off the job invariably affect performance on the job. For example, if creditors are pressuring an employee who is having difficulty meeting financial obligations, he is likely to be worried to the point that he spends even his work time trying to figure out a way to improve his situation or otherwise solve the problem. Just the fact that the employee is occupied enough with the problem to bring it to his superior's attention is an indication that his work is being affected. This is, in itself, a clear sign of a need for intervention on the manager's part.

Providing guidance to the staff is a way of helping them carry their burdens like Christ carried our sins to the cross. "We who are strong ought to bear with the failings of the weak, and not to please ourselves; let each of us please his neighbor for his good, to edify him" (Rom. 15:1-2). When we edify one another we are building each other up, helping each to grow in strength so that we can better face the problem we must deal with.

By helping the employee bear his burden through counseling, the manager is not trying to solve the problem for him or to take the problem on himself. The manager's job is to listen, to advise, to offer suggestions to help the other person to come to terms with self, thereby becoming receptive to a solution. The counselor is not himself a healer but serves as a facilitator in the healing process. Jesus alone is the healer.

For example, when counseling an employee about excessive drinking the manager cannot solve the alcoholic's problem by taking it away from him or by simply telling him to stop drinking. What the manager can do is provide support for the employee. He can pray with and for him. He can encourage him and be available to listen any time he needs strengthening to overcome temptation. He can help by ministering the forgiveness Christ has earned for each of us. In essence, the manager must show the employee that he is loved and that someone is willing to take the time to help. Just the knowledge that someone cares can have a healing effect and can free the person with the problem enough for him to be led to Christ, the source of all solutions.

Counsel is important and of much value. The Book of Proverbs is filled with admonitions to seek and accept counsel. A few such Scriptures are:

He who heeds instruction is on the path to life, but he who rejects reproof goes astray. (Prov. 10:17)

The way of a fool is right in his own eyes, but a wise man listens to advice. (Prov. 12:15)

Listen to advice and accept instruction, that you may gain wisdom for the future. (Prov. 19:20)

Even though these words are true, how does the manager convince his employees of the wisdom of seeking counsel? First, he gives them an example. He must openly and willingly seek the advice of both superiors and subordinates. Then, having received this counsel, he must prove his confidence in it by weighing it and acting on that which he finds useful.

Second, the counsel he gives must be wise and practical. Lofty platitudes and theories are not counsel, they are cop-outs. When an employee comes seeking advice about a marital problem, he should receive concrete advice on how to improve his marriage, not a detailed theology of marriage. It must be gentle and directed toward encouraging the person to find and implement the solution to the problem. The best way to insure the wisdom of this advice is to measure it according to God's Word.

Third, the manager must be available when his counsel is needed. An employee may unexpectedly bring him a problem in the middle of the day or while he is at home during off hours. He needs to respond at these times despite what his personal preference might be. With patience he must listen to the person and discern whether emergency counseling is necessary or if it can be scheduled at a more convenient time. If it needs to be dealt with immediately, the counseling situation must take priority over what else is scheduled. If, after the initial conversation, the manager feels the problem can best be handled by a scheduled appointment, he needs to advise the employee of this, schedule a time, and be available at that time. All this takes time and patience but if the manager wants his people to come to him with their problems he must take care to be available when he is needed.

By his example, the provision of good advice, and by being available, the manager will build the confidence and trust of his staff. This will bring them to him when in need so that he can minister as the Lord leads him. Through the manager, Jesus can be brought to the staff, meeting them at the point of their need.

By providing gentle, concerned counseling, the manager shows the employees the love of Christ through his interest. Most problems are at least partially of a spiritual nature and the Christian manager is equipped to deal with these. He has the Word of God and the guiding Holy Spirit dwelling in him. Only with divine wisdom will he know how to meet his employees' needs. Those who counsel without manifesting the love of Christ are not capable of reaching into the spirit of the person they are working with.

Christian managers do not have to be professional counselors but they must learn to be useful in counseling. They must learn to discern the nature of a problem or need and how to deal with the situation. Many times the manager will be able to provide all the help the person needs but he must also be able to recognize his own limitations and know where to lead the person for help he cannot effectively give.

To be able to provide effective guidance, the manager must be focused on Jesus, relying on the Holy Spirit to lead him in helping others find solutions to their problems. In all of its forms counseling is an essential function of the manager. In helping to meet the concerns of his staff and by leading them to the resolution of their problems, he helps them to be properly concerned with their work. This helps to make the organization more effective and productive.

Teaching and Instruction

All of us can probably agree with certainty that we continue to learn as long as we live. There is so much to the fulness of the Christian life that there is always something new to understand, some different insight or illumination. One place where we must particularly be open to learning is at work and there it is most often that the employee learns from his supervisor, his manager.

To be a manager is to be a teacher. He must be able to instruct his staff in the performance of their jobs. He needs to show them how to improve what they are doing and teach them new procedures. Rather than actually doing the work himself it is the manager's task to teach his employees how to be more productive.

But the manager's responsibility to teach goes beyond instruction on the performance of technical or administrative tasks. The Christian manager must also instruct his staff about what it means to live a victorious Christian life. The question we must seek to answer is: How does he do it?

To help us understand this we must reflect for a moment on the teaching ministry of Christ. Jesus taught His disciples and in the way He instructed them we can learn how to teach our employees.

Three of the methods Jesus used in teaching are of particular interest to us. He expounded and brought insight into the Word of God; He gave practical illustrations of the things He taught (i.e. the parables); and He lived as an example of how to do what He imparted in His teaching.

For the manager the most important of these teaching tools is example. By living in accord with God's Word and remaining steadfast in the truth, the manager is providing teaching about how to live as a Christian. Also, the way a manager handles himself in certain situations will teach his staff. For example, if you are having a problem with gossip and backbiting in the office, you should offer counsel concerning the seriousness of the problem, indicating how it injures all involved and is as vicious an action as physical violence (Matt. 5:21-22). This is instruction in the ways of the Lord and improves staff relationships at the same time.

Example alone is not enough. The staff must be aware of the nature of the life style the manager has chosen to live. They must have an understanding of what it means to be a Christian and this knowledge comes through learning the Word of God. The manager can teach the Word in several ways. One is by establishing a noon-hour Bible study. This will reach out to those who are already hungry for the Word or are looking for an answer that they think they might find in the study group. Probably, most of those who come to such sessions will already be believers and it is here that the manager has an excellent opportunity to "feed the sheep."

Another way of imparting the truth of Scripture is by informal sharing at coffee break or whenever the opportunity presents itself. Often something will come up in a conversation to which appropriate Scripture or Bible truth can be addressed. For example, if the discussion is about the way the President of the United States is handling foreign policy in the Middle East, the insertion of a biblical perspective on events can prove to be most enlightening to even the nonbelievers who are engaged in the conversation. If the manager is open to hear what the Spirit is saying and is willing to speak the Word of the Lord to his staff, he might be surprised at how many of the staff are hungry for the Word, and at the same time he will provide other Christians with an opportunity to share with and feed him.

Jesus made very effective use of parables to illustrate the principles He was teaching. From our life experience we can all draw on things that have happened that were used by God to teach us something or to reveal a truth to us. By using anecdotes to illustrate what we teach we lend a measure of validity to the principle. For example, if we teach what God says about submission to authority only by using Bible references, it is difficult to see the practical application of the teaching. But, if we make the lesson come alive with testimony and examples of the blessing that comes when we recognize the authority God has established and submit to it, the students begin to see that it is possible. The manager should use illustrations whether teaching spiritual principles or on practical matters. These illuminating anecdotes can be used as part of a formal Bible lesson as well as part of routine conversation. In either way they help to make the Word of God clearer for the listener.

In sum, the manager should never forget that he is also a teacher of the principles of Christian living. It is precisely because he finds himself immersed in the same situation as his employees that he is a most effective instrument for God to use to bring forth His message to them. By virtue of his position and the respect the staff has for him he will often be heard by those who would not otherwise receive the Word.

Summary

Discipline, reward, counsel and teaching are all part of the manager's responsibility. The way he carries out these tasks is crucial to the development of his relationship with his employees. As a Christian he must seek to fairly apply God's revealed will to each activity, to each situation. He can only minister to the spiritual needs of his staff during the course of his job by submitting these tasks to God and doing them in His will.

15

Ministry to Yourself

And great multitudes gathered to hear and to be
healed of their infirmities. But he withdrew to the
wilderness and prayed. (Luke 5:15-16)

Jesus spent most of His time ministering to the needs of
the huge crowds that would gather around Him. His
mission was exhausting and He knew He regained
strength by resting in the presence of His Father. Jesus
understood that He could not effectively minister if He
did not allow the Father to minister to Him.

Most managers will agree that theirs is not an easy job.
There are deadlines to be met, complaints to be
investigated, problems to be solved, and critical decisions
with long-reaching effects to be made. This pressure,
these demands, often cause the manager to neglect
himself as he is busy tending to his job and meeting the
needs of his staff.

Failure to care for yourself is failure to do your job
properly. Unless the manager is in excellent physical,
mental and spiritual health he will not be able to do what is
expected of him. Thomas Merton wrote:

There are times, then, when in order to keep ourselves in existence at all we simply have to sit back for a while and do nothing. And for a man who has let himself be drawn completely out of himself by his activity, nothing is more difficult than to sit still and rest, doing nothing at all. The very act of resting is the hardest and most courageous act he can perform: and often it is quite beyond his power.[1]

While it might be beyond the power of man it is not beyond the power of Christ to give us peace in the midst of turmoil. This chapter is concerned with how every manager must learn to allow the Lord to minister to him and lead him to spiritual peace. In our ever-busy, modern world it is not easy to passively allow Jesus to wash our feet as He did those of His first disciples. But it is necessary and the following are a few suggestions about how it can be done.

You Are Not Alone

A first step toward the appropriation of this peace is to realize you do not have to face your problems alone and that your burdens are jointly borne by others.

Of course, Jesus is always with you, but our focus here is on the other people in your life: your spouse, children, friends, those you fellowship with regularly. If you do not recognize the importance of these others away from your job and plan to regularly spend time with them, to share your life with them, you will not be able to put your work aside and let Jesus minister His peace to you.

How do these others help to bring you to a peaceful place? First, they provide you with a focal point outside of

[1]Thomas Merton, *No Man Is An Island* (New York: Harcourt, Brace & World, Inc., 1955), p. 123.

your work environment. There is your son's little league practice, your daughter's piano recital, your wife's menu planning and they all need your full attention. These things provide an opportunity to leave the job behind at the office, to put it out of mind until you must return to it.

Second, the Lord often ministers to us through the fellowship of others. Just being with a family or friends and sharing in a common experience like a picnic or dinner can bring the peace and comfort of Christ to us.

In sharing our lives with others outside the job we can put aside the pressures and problems that demand so much of our time and attention each week. We need this diversion and the rest that is ministered through it. To become addicted to our work and say we do not need this peace is to deny Christ by saying we can do it all on our own power. It is both wrong and dangerous.

Be Not Anxious

When faced with problems it is easy to become anxious, to become worried about whether or not things will work out in a satisfactory way. We worry about the accuracy of the estimated financing needed to purchase new equipment. We worry about the new accountant we have hired and the accuracy of the vital reports he is responsible for. The world's way is to worry about the matter until it is resolved or becomes a bigger problem to worry about. But Jesus said, "Let not your hearts be troubled; believe in God, believe also in me" (John 14:1).

The Lord tells us not to worry but to trust Him to guide us in all things. He says if we have faith in the Father and in Him we have no reason to be anxious. We must learn to act obediently on these words. The anxiety in our lives blocks the work of the Savior in us by focusing our attention on the problem and not Christ. The tension must be released to make room for the Lord.

Life is never like a ride in a sleek sailboat on a placid lake. Troubles, illness and other trials are faced by everyone. It is important and necessary to understand that we will be faced with these difficulties as part of our Christian lives. The apostle Peter knew very well the trials of a life of service to the gospel. With this understanding he wrote: "Beloved, do not be surprised at the fiery ordeal which comes upon you to prove you, as though something strange were happening to you. But rejoice in so far as you share Christ's sufferings, that you may also rejoice and be glad when his glory is revealed" (1 Pet. 4:12-13).

Worry can harm us physically and spiritually. Stomach ulcers, high blood pressure and many forms of mental illness are the result of anxiety. We can become so burdened that our faith is shaken and our defenses against evil are weakened.

God loves us and does not want us to be harmed by disquiet in our inner man. Therefore, the Lord has said and speaks to us now, "Have I not commanded you? Be strong and of good courage; be not frightened, neither be dismayed; for the Lord your God is with you wherever you go" (Josh. 1:9).

If we are to overcome the strain and tension that worry brings with it we must strengthen ourselves to obey the Father's command. The first requirements are an open heart and a sincere desire to do the will of God. This means understanding that God loves us so much that He gave us His only Son to save us from sin. If we understand this we can trust the Lord to help us in all things. Peace comes when we remember how much God loves us and that we should never allow fear and doubt to hinder our reliance on Him.

Jesus Christ brought love and eternal life to mankind. In doing so, He overcame all things that result from the original sin, including worry. He provides us with the proper way to face all difficulties. Freedom from anxiety comes when we believe and act on God's Word, "Peace I leave with you; my peace I give to you; not as the world gives do I give to you. Let not your hearts be troubled, neither let them be afraid" (John 14:27).

Having placed our trust in God and received the peace of Christ into our hearts, there is one more step that is necessary to cement in place the serenity we have found. Prayer is the adhesive that binds us to God, enabling us to maintain a peaceful and unworried heart. In any situation, regardless of how insignificant it may seem, we must turn our burdens over to the Lord, believing He will hear and answer. "Call to me and I will answer you, and will tell you great and hidden things which you have not known" (Jer. 33:3).

We must place our full trust in God and call upon His power for strength and wisdom so we do not allow worry to open the way for Satan's forces. We cannot hesitate in applying these teachings of the Scriptures to our daily lives and allow the comforting serenity of Christ Jesus to surround us always.

Resting with the Lord*

Above we said we must pray because peace comes in prayer. As we get to know people by spending time with them, we come to know God by spending time with Him in the communion of prayer. To find the time and place can be difficult but the manager must be able to be alone with

*This section is adapted from an article, "Antidote for Actionmania" which appeared in *New Covenant*, July 1977, and is used by permission.

the Lord and experience His rest if he or she is to have the strength necessary to do the job.

A sense of urgency is characteristic of every facet of modern life. From family reunions to church activities we are controlled by schedules that allow little time for rest. At home we bolt down instant meals as we become immersed in a television show or before we dive into a hobby. At the office we rush between appointments and conduct business over lunch to save time. Even when our bodies are at rest, we are afraid we will miss something if we empty our minds or momentarily close them to the endless streams of stimuli that speed toward us.

This pace can adversely affect our health. High blood pressure, ulcers, nervous disorders and emotional problems are the effects of a hyperactive life. To keep up we find it necessary to take stimulants, and we rely on alcohol and drugs to slow us down.

Often the turbulence blinds us and we must be forced to see what this life style can do to us. It was not until after several years of clawing my way up through the ranks of bureaucracy that I reluctantly took the time for a complete physical examination, including eight days in the hospital to determine why so young a man had hypertension. This enforced inactivity gave me the opportunity to reflect on the hurried nature of my existence. I had no choice but to be patient, to wait, to rest. Within three days my blood pressure was within normal ranges and the knots in my stomach had disappeared.

But it is not only our physical health that is impaired. The urgency of our lives can make us too busy to love others and serve them. Husbands and wives, parents and children fail to communicate because they must rush off to attend business appointments, parent-teacher meetings, or social events. As a result, divorce rates soar and delinquency problems are out of control.

It was this sort of thing that led Blaise Pascal to reflect: "All the troubles of life come upon us because we refuse to sit quietly for a while each day in our rooms."[2]

Spirit-led Christians can be caught up in this cycle too, even to the extent of neglecting God. The clamor of the daily race draws our attention from Him, and our spirits become victims of the sense of urgency. Like the poet, John Donne, we have all had occasion to "neglect God and his angels for the noise of a fly, for the rattling of a coach, for the whining of a door."[3] And even when we do serve the Lord, we often lack an understanding of what it means to rest before Him.

I know of a young man who exhausted himself in his zeal to do the Lord's work. One evening, he arrived late at a prayer meeting with his tie askew and his eyes red and sunken. When someone asked why he looked so bad he smiled and said that, besides putting in a full day's work, he had made twenty-three visits for the Lord. At this, one woman ventured, "But how many did God want you to see?" The young man was insulted by the question but it gnawed at him until he came before the Lord, seeking an answer. The next time the group met, he humbly related what the Lord had impressed on him: he needed to visit only two.

With all this pressure to be constantly busy, is it possible to pull out of the mainstream, stop rushing about, and be renewed? Yoga, transcendental meditation and golf are three of the world's heralded cures for man's "actionmania." While these techniques may relax the body and mind they fail to renew the man completely

2Quoted in Wirt, ed., *Living Quotations For Christians*, op. cit., p. 194.
3Ibid., p. 153.

because they do not give rest to the spiritual part of us. Only when the spirit is refreshed can the body and mind fully enjoy the healing that pure relaxation brings. Hobbies, sleep and medication can help the body and the mind rest, but the spirit, the part of us that is most like God, can only be refreshed through the loving power we experience in God's presence.

In the fourth chapter of the letter to the Hebrews the author compares rest to being in God's presence: "So there is a full complete rest still waiting for the people of God. Christ has already entered there. He is resting from this work, just as God did after the creation" (Heb. 4:9-10 TLB).

It is, then, when we are in perfect communion with the Lord, that we experience complete rest. Though we are still confined to our mortal state we can experience an incomplete, yet appetizing taste of God's rest. It was to accomplish this that the Father commanded us to cease from labor and honor Him on the sabbath (Exod. 20:8-11). Honoring God through worship, thanksgiving and praise is communion with our Creator. Thus, inherent in this command is the divinely-ordained relationship between rest and communion with God.

To be renewed, the whole person—body, mind and spirit—must be rested. Before I came to know Jesus as Savior I would come home from the office, mentally exhausted, and have a drink or two before dinner. By the time I finished eating I was ready for bed and, despite long hours of sleep, I always awoke without feeling refreshed. Now, when I come home seeking relief from tension a few moments alone before my Lord is preparation for an evening's study, worship or recreation with my family. The job is still tiring and I probably get less sleep, but now I have learned to relax my spirit as God wants.

Our spirit is meant to be the controlling part of our person. As its renewal brings the body and mind into a deeper state of relaxation our burdens are lifted and our spirit reclines in the arms of a Lord who offers: "Come to me, all who labor and are heavy laden, and I will give you rest. Take my yoke upon you, and learn from me; for I am gentle and lowly in heart, and you will find rest for your souls" (Matt. 11:28-29). By accepting the peacefulness the Lord has made ready for us, we mature and are brought closer to Him, opening ourselves up to Him as vessels ready to do His will.

Before we can share in these blessings of tranquility, though, we must learn to listen to the Holy Spirit. We are attentive to the noises of the world, but how often do we listen for God's voice? We may speak to Him regularly in prayer, but too often without heeding the command: "Incline your ear, and come to me; hear, that your soul may live" (Isa. 55:3). If we desire to be in God's presence we must obey His will, but we cannot know His will unless we listen to Him in our spirit.

It took a problem at work to teach me what can happen, even at the human level, if we fail to listen. Despite my lengthy instructions concerning his various tasks, one of my staff members would frequently submit incomplete assignments. I noticed, however, that he always did a thorough job on work he initiated himself. I finally understood this discrepancy when I learned of his difficulty with listening attentively; this employee failed because he never completely knew what I expected. We have a similar problem in our relationship with God.

We should not be so attentive to the world as to let

God's voice go unnoticed. As a boy, the prophet Samuel did not realize the voice he heard calling him was the Lord's. Not understanding that God would speak directly to him, Samuel answered Eli, the priest, three times. Unlike Samuel, we should expect to hear God's voice. The Lord calls to us in our hearts and in our spirits. We must be able to recognize when He is speaking to us so we may answer, as Samuel finally did, "Speak, for thy servant hears" (1 Sam. 3:10).

Being in God's rest also means we are freed of our anxieties and have learned to wait patiently before Him as Scripture frequently exhorts: "Be still before the Lord, and wait patiently for him" (Ps. 37:7). "Wait for the Lord; be strong, and let your heart take courage; yea, wait for the Lord!" (Ps. 27:14). Such reminders are important because we dislike waiting and want to rush God into acting on our behalf. We lift our needs to Him expecting an immediate response and, if we fail to see an immediate answer, our faith wavers. Because of these erroneous expectations, learning to wait on the Lord can be a painful experience.

For example, the first time I attended a prayer meeting, I felt I should move right into a leadership role. I wanted to serve the Lord in the front ranks, just like I do in the government agency I work for. Instead of waiting for the Lord to assign this responsibility to me, I sought it on my own behalf. But, as I tried to work with the community leaders, I was disarmed by the loving way in which these wiser and more mature Christians discerned my problem and counseled me on learning to be humble. This particular door closed. Then I considered the possibility of leading a Bible study, but scheduling conflicts arose before I could volunteer. Finally, after some other deflating experiences, I prayed, "Father, use me as you will. I'll be patient and wait for you to use me." It was shortly after I stopped interfering and started waiting that opportunities for me to serve the Lord began to develop.

This experience taught me that we cannot hurry the Lord but that we must act according to His schedule. When we realize this, we can cast away our worries and wait patiently for Him.

Understanding what it means to rest before God is an important step, but it is not enough for one who desires to be obedient to the Father's will. We must build upon the foundation of Scripture and, in the midst of a distracting world, search for and find blessed stillness.

When I first came to Jesus, I spent many hours in prayer and Bible study trying to come closer to Him. For a while my spirit was adequately fed by this and Christian fellowship, but soon I could sense a void in my soul similar to the one I feel when I am away from my family for a day. I could read God's Word and I could speak to Him, but the closeness, the communion I sought, was not fully satisfying. When I discovered how to experience God's rest, the emptiness was filled as I began to grow closer to my Savior.

To feel this communion I try to make a habit of sitting quietly before God each day. I try to get out of bed earlier than I must and begin my day with prayer, asking for guidance and thanking God for His blessings. I select a passage or two of Scripture which I carefully read and reflect on, thinking how the words apply to me. Finally, in those quiet, early morning moments before my children race from their rooms, I sit alone on the floor, close my eyes and imagine myself sitting before Jesus. It is this quiet time that refreshes me and prepares me to go out to do the Lord's work during the day. For a few precious moments I sit back, open up my soul, and strive to listen to God.

He never speaks to me with a thundering voice or from a burning bush; but He speaks. I am afraid that many times I miss His words because I am too involved with what is around me, but when I hear Him I am filled and guided by His mercy and love.

All of us need to determine the way that best suits our own situation and allows us to enter daily into the Lord's rest and to listen to God. As He speaks we will hear words of guidance, love, encouragement, and correction. We will find that this intermission in our busy lives will refresh and renew our spirits. "They who wait for the Lord shall renew their strength, they shall mount up with wings like eagles, they shall run and not be weary, they shall walk and not faint" (Isa. 40:31). This strength will carry us through each day's trials.

We are too weak and ignorant to win in the spiritual war that rages about us without God's rest and the guidance that comes through it. But with them, we will bear sweet fruit; we will be better able to love the Lord, to obey Him, to cleave to Him, and to serve Him.

The manager's responsibility to self is met by making a serious effort to spend time with the Lord and with others away from work and related matters. This time is more valuable to the job than those extra hours would be if spent behind the desk or in the plant. Even the strongest of us tire physically and mentally. When we are overworked, our thinking processes become less effective and we are more liable to make mistakes. Therefore,

Ministry To Yourself

proper rest helps to improve our work. The rested and refreshed manager will be able to more effectively do his job, accomplishing more in the time allotted for it. The costs of ignoring this ministry to ourselves far exceed the benefits of the extra attention to work. To be valuable to our employer, to be of service to the Lord, to be able to help others, we need to learn to receive the ministry that strengthens us for these tasks.

16

The Fruit of
Christian Management

He who plants and he who waters are equal, and each
shall receive his wages according to his labor. (1 Cor.
3:8)

A disciple is not meant to carry on the empty and
meaningless activity of the world, but is to bear fruit that
glorifies God. Jesus tells each of us, "You did not choose
me, but I chose you and appointed you that you should go
and bear fruit and that your fruit should abide" (John
15:16). All the Christian manager does in his job should
bring forth fruit, for this is the purpose of his service to
God and man.

If we truly love God and seek Him above all things we
will obey Him. This obedience is rewarded by our loving
Father because it originates in love and not through
compulsion. We are free to obey or not, we can make the
choice and the motivating factor will be our love of God or
the lack of it.

Thus, if the Christian manager seeks to obey God by
truly being a shepherd to his staff and applying the
teachings of the Word in his job, he should expect that his

efforts will be fruitful. The Bible promises:

"If you walk in my statutes and observe my commandments and do them, then I will give you your rains in their season, and the land shall yield its increase, and the trees of the field shall yield their fruit. . . . And I will make my abode among you, and my soul shall not abhor you. And I will walk among you, and will be your God, and you shall be my people." (Lev. 26:3-4, 11-12)

The Essential Seed

The very essence of fruit-bearing in Christian management is found in the truth that the manager does not earn the fruit but submits himself to Jesus so that the fruit may be borne. "I am the vine, you are the branches. He who abides in me, and I in him, he it is that bears much fruit, for apart from me you can do nothing" (John 15:5).

The presence of Christ in the life of the manager creates a foundation of love out of which the manager's concern and honest desire to serve his staff must grow. Christ's presence in us brings forth the wisdom and understanding that is necessary to discern what actions should be and must be taken. Jesus provides the firm foundation on which we can securely build.

This is the seed of the fruit borne by the Christian manager: that he willingly turns his life, his job, over to Jesus, knowing that His is the best way and that Christ will work through him. The manager recognizes that he is spiritually impoverished and can be rich only when he surrenders himself as an empty vessel to be filled by Christ and guided by the Holy Spirit according to the will of the Father.

Concrete and Not-So-Concrete Results

Two types of fruit are borne in the practice of Christian management, the concrete or temporal and the spiritual. The temporal are the practical successes and improvements that come about when the manager understands his calling. It is these temporal, measurable results that will be of greatest interest to the world and it is the manager's responsibility to give God the credit He is due for these successes. The temporal fruits not only benefit the organization through improved operations but they also provide witness to the practicality of God's Word and His interest in our every endeavor. Following are some thoughts and examples on how the application of God's wisdom to management tasks brings success.

All managers are decision-makers and God's wisdom is essential to the making of good decisions. Almost every action they take is the result of a decision. It is on the decisions of managers that the success or failure of an operation depends. The wisdom with which he makes his choices will be the critical factor in whether or not the manager is competent in his job.

The key to sound decision-making is to learn what God says about the situation you are faced with. Joshua and the men of Israel made an alliance with the Gibeonites without consulting the Lord. They were deceived into sparing a heathen nation they had been directed to destroy and they made themselves vulnerable to the pagan influences of those people, their submission to which ultimately brought punishment upon the Israelites (Josh. 9).

We can avoid such disastrous results by taking the decision to the Lord, for "He shows how to distinguish right from wrong, how to find the right decision every time" (Prov. 2:9 TLB). By admitting that we need the Lord's help, turning to Him in prayer and checking what His Word says about the matter, we are open to receiving His direction.

I was recently faced with a major decision about what should be done with my job. Though I was the head of a division I felt there was a more effective way to organize the staff, combining another position with mine. In effect, I had to decide whether or not to organize myself out of a job and ask my supervisor to look for a place where I could be utilized. I prayed about it, sought the counsel of others, and looked to see what the Scriptures said about it. As the Spirit led me through the Word I began to understand, in a fresh way, that God wants us to do our jobs to the best of our ability, as though we are working for Him (Eph. 6:5-8). To me this meant that if I failed to report the findings of my organization studies, even though it might cost me my job, I would not be obedient to God.

With His guidance I was comfortable with pointing this out to the department head. This resulted in a shifting of responsibility that allowed the division to operate more efficiently and, at the same time, to use me more effectively. According to man's wisdom I would have done all I could to save what I had. If I had done so I would have remained unhappy, unchallenged and unfulfilled in my work.

The most critical decisions and/or problems faced by a manager arise in the context of organizing and staffing, in dealing with people. It is management's task to place people where they are best utilized and most productive. This is generally where they are happiest and relate well with those around them. Determining where such places are, whether in hiring the new employee, reassigning staff, trying to solve personnel disputes, or finding solutions to production bottlenecks, is as difficult as it is important.

Deciding how to utilize a person will have an effect on every aspect of his life as well as the performance of the organization. For example, placing an experienced engineer in a drafting position not only fails to fully use his skills, but it also will not challenge the engineer, causing even this less complicated work to be below the quality desired. A lack of enthusiasm for the job may develop and carry over into a despondent family life in which the individual grows in feelings of uselessness.

In an opposite situation, such as placing an untrained person in a position requiring accounting knowledge or expecting a file clerk to do the typing of a senior secretary, the employee will not have the skills to do the job and can be easily discouraged by not being able to adequately do the assigned task. Again, the feeling of failure that can be generated from such a situation is likely to extend into the individual's relationships and activities away from work.

It is a fruit of Christian management to be able to manage people, not as objects, but with love and compassion, as fellow human beings. With the understanding of Christ and the discernment imparted by the Holy Spirit, the manager is better prepared to assess the needs and the spiritual condition of his staff.

From this perspective, and in prayer, the manager can determine whether or not the person he is concerned with will fit in a given place and whether that assignment will benefit the organization. Also, this discernment helps the manager understand the underlying causes of personal performance. Once the situation is understood he can look for a solution.

In sum, the manager is to treat his staff as Jesus would care for them. A reading of the Gospels quickly reveals the fruit that came forth simply as a result of Christ's loving relationships with everyone. This love is manifest in the management situation by free and useful communication, eagerness to cooperate and help one another, willingness to listen to advice and to seek it. It is in this love than an atmosphere of cooperation is created that is not charged with the anxieties that pride and self-centeredness cause.

A love-filled atmosphere at work can bring about dramatic results. People are happier and have fewer problems. If they have problems they know that others at work care about them and will help them in their need. All this adds up to improved production and better-quality work.

Spiritual Fruit

As the Lord takes control of the work place, He is active in the hearts of the people involved. Through the example and witness of the manager, spiritual needs are met, lives are changed and people come into the kingdom of God. It is inevitable that if the manager freely shares his commitment to Christ he will arouse the interest of those he works with. Some responses will be critical and negative but more often he will be faced with people who are searching—non-Christians searching for a new life, or Christians searching for a new dimension, a second touch to lift them from spiritual stagnation and bring them out of their apathy.

As Christ becomes real to the staff more people will begin to examine their lives. Some will come to know the

Lord for the first time, others will be led to a closer walk with Jesus. Defeated lives will become victorious lives. There will be a more open sharing of needs when others know they can receive the help and comfort they need. Staff will spend free time sharing the Lord with one another and will begin praying for and with each other. As the Lord begins to work and gradually is given first place in the lives of more and more people a revival can begin to take place in the organization.

As I became more open about my relationship with Christ and began to try to be obedient to Him in my job, I saw these very things begin to happen to my staff. I only provided a witness and a vessel the Lord could use. All of my staff has not dramatically come to Christ as Savior but changes have been visible enough that a non-Christian in the department has given the newly gathered core of Christians the nickname: "God Squad." We certainly have the attention of those we work with and are daily growing in unity, despite diverse denominational backgrounds. Needs are being met and outsiders are beginning to look at our lives with interest. We have not yet produced a bumper crop of fruit but there is promise of a rich harvest.

One measure of what is beginning to happen is the degree to which attitudes toward work and the work place are changing. For those in Christian fellowship at the office, even though at times the work may be burdensome and unchallenging, there is a new understanding that they are doing what God wants them to do. They are beginning to see that they are really working for God through their service to the organization. In addition, the office is no longer viewed by these same people as primarily a place of drudgery but as a place where Jesus is alive and the fellowship of other Christians can be found.

Thus they have a new reason for coming to work, a reason that keeps them coming even on those mornings they used to call in "sick." All this is resulting in the creation of a work climate that is more agreeable and desirable. At present only a few people have made and are experiencing these changes, but if only one person comes to know Jesus in a richer, more personal way through my ministry as a manager, then I know I have been successful as a fruit-bearing branch of the vine that is Christ.

17

Bringing Christ
into the Organization

Unless the Lord builds the house, those who build it
labor in vain. (Ps. 127:1)

In this chapter I hope to draw on my limited experience
to develop some thoughts on the practicality of bringing
Christ into the organization. The intent is not to present
the reader with a recipe or step-by-step approach, but
with some ideas that will serve as seed. Even with a
century of experience it would be difficult to do more, for
each situation is different and must be handled as the
Lord directs. This is why He must be the builder, not the
manager who serves as His instrument. The organization
cannot be "Christianized" by man's weak ideas and
according to man's fancy. When the crusaders of the
Middle Ages tried to return Christianity to the Holy Land
by the power of the sword they failed. The manager,
likewise, will fail if he tries to force Christ on his
employees by virtue of his position. If Christ is truly to
become central to the existence of the organization, the
Lord himself must be the architect as well as the
construction foreman. Each such institution will grow

according to the plan ordained by God if it is to be built at all.

The Christ-Centered Organization

For the purposes of this study we will refer to that organizational unit in which the manager makes Jesus welcome, as a Christ-centered organization. The Christ-centered organization is a unit of people working under the direction of a Christian manager for the achievement of a common goal or set of goals, and is guided in its operations by God's Word as revealed and taught to us by the Holy Spirit.

It can be comprised of a staff of any size from a manager and his secretary to a large company, and not all the individuals on the staff will necessarily be Christians. At the least, a nucleus of believers will be the "salt of the organization," exerting influence on the conduct of the organization's affairs. It is from the Christians in the institution that love and obedience to God flows forth, touching all others.

We must be sure to keep in mind that the quality of the commitment to Christ is more important than the quantity as expressed in a large number of employees paying only lip service to the Lord. The manager should never fall into the trap of measuring the organization's level of Christianity by sheer numbers. The only way the organization really grows is as dedicated, single-hearted disciples lead others to this vital relationship with Christ, building a community of believers within the institutional structure.

While it is not essential that the community form under the shepherding of the manager, the Spirit of God will probably flow more freely when one in an authoritative and leadership position is a believer. When the manager lives according to the Word and implicity requires his staff to conduct its business in a way that is acceptable to God, even non-Christians come under the authority of Christ. For the manager and Christian staff, the Word, both written and incarnate, is explicitly the final authority in all matters.

In all cases the people in the organization work together to achieve the goals assigned to them. For the Christ-centered institution these goals go beyond those of production, cost control, sales and the like. They must include the goal of serving God by allowing Him to transform the staff into living witnesses of His power. In other words, the ultimate goal of the Christian establishment would be to support each employee's ability to perform his or her job by leading them to a closer relationship with God, through Jesus Christ.

If the organization is to achieve its goals the people who comprise it must be coordinated and directed by a manager who perceives his role as pastoral as well as managerial. It is this person who is the focus of the integration of work with discipleship and it is essentially he who is the catalyst in the building of the Christ-centered organization.

Building Blocks

The spiritual growth of an organization requires a firm commitment on the part of the manager. If there are other Christians on his staff, he should enlist their commitment and support.

The work begins with prayer, prayer for the staff, for the Christians at work to grow closer to Christ, prayer for the salvation of the others. Prayer is the support necessary to effectively utilize the other building blocks of fellowship, oral witness, and witness through example. In prayer, the manager and staff can seek and receive the guidance they need to understand how to properly minister and witness in their specific situation.

The Christians in the organization must fellowship as brothers and sisters in the Lord. This can include informal sharing, spontaneous prayer together, or a formalized Bible study or prayer meeting. In this fellowship the nucleus will grow in the strength and grow in the unity needed to spread the good news of Christ throughout the organization. Personal and corporate needs can be addressed and prayed about, victories and trials shared, and an opportunity provided to commit oneself to the others in the group. With God's guidance this fellowship will grow into a natural and critically important part of the work day.

Prayer and fellowship strengthen the Christian to live the life of Christ in the face of the trials the world brings on him. By providing a witness in action, others in the organization have an opportunity to see what it is to be a Christian, and the way is paved for the sharing of the gospel with nonbelievers on the staff.

The Christian organization is built on the witness to Christ that plants the seeds which the Holy Spirit nurtures and draws others to the Father through Jesus. It is this witness which the Lord uses to touch the hearts of the nonbelievers so that He can transform them into children of the kingdom, building the body of Christ at the same time as the organization. To be effective, this witness must rest upon a firm foundation of prayer and strengthening fellowship.

An Example

No one can produce a model that can be applied to every institution. Just as God works differently in each life, He works in unique ways with each manager's staff. Despite these limitations, examples can be helpful. So, with this in mind, I will briefly share what the Lord has been doing in the office I work in.

When I took my present position I knew that at least eight or nine of the thirty people on my staff were Christians, though only one ever regularly shared his convictions with me. The Lord was in our lives but not in our work.

As I began to talk with this brother we began to see the need for a fellowship among the believers we worked with. The Lord used me to lead him into a closer walk through the baptism in the Holy Spirit. Then, with the two of us and the transfer of a Christian woman to my staff, we formed a nucleus and the gates were opened for the sharing of Christ's love.

Our fellowship soon grew to four when my secretary was brought closer to the cross. Gradually we found that despite denominational differences, we spoke the same language and loved the same Savior. We began to trust and confide in one another more and, occasionally, pray together. Part of this growth together was the perception of the need to extend our love and service to the rest of the division staff and into the remainder of the department. This led us to the establishment of a noon-hour Bible study that once a week draws together from five to ten Christians from throughout the department, and is now beginning to reach out to those in other departments.

The Bible study serves as a focal point for the growth of the Christ-centered organization primarily in our division, but also is being used to plant seeds in other areas of the city administrative structure. It has provided a new and needed channel for fellowship and is the base from which we began to more freely share the Lord with others. Now, our fellowship is no longer confined to once a week, but is spontaneous.

In the process we have become aware of many others in the department who are not so open but are beginning to be reached. Christians are gradually identifying themselves to one another and are becoming freer to share beyond the requirements at work. I am often blessed when someone who normally does not freely speak of spiritual things comes by my office to tell me of a prayer need or to share what the Lord is doing in his or her life.

While the core group is small it has been used by the Lord to awaken other Christians to their need for fellowship and the availability of it. It has also awakened new desires in the brethren to share Christ with those they work with who have not yet met Him. I do not know if any have come to Jesus through this witness but I do know that God's Word is being proclaimed and Christ's love is being poured out in the department. The organization is perceptibly changing as God's presence becomes real to more people.

To this point I believe that the real growth has been inside the believers in the department and their relationships with one another. We are growing in unity. We are growing in a sense of mission and in power to carry out that mission. And this growth is expressed in the increased frequency of prayer with and for one another, and the more intense ministry some are involved in at the office.

In sum, the awareness that Christ is active in our work has heightened and this is creating an environment that is being bathed with His light. As the light becomes brighter it is becoming more difficult for it to be ignored. Jesus has been invited in and He is taking charge of the organization!

18

A Warning:
Pitfalls to Avoid

There is a way which seems right to a man, but its end
is the way to death. (Prov. 14:12)

In the last chapter we examined some of the signs of the
growing presence of Christ within an organization. While
it is most desirable that the staff become increasingly
Christ-centered and Spirit-led, there is a right way as
well as a wrong way for the manager to go about the task
of bringing Jesus into his work.

The correct way is to allow the Holy Spirit to use and
direct him according to the Lord's timing and plan. Most
of this book is an elaboration on the correct method. The
wrong way results when the manager, full of zeal to
preach the Gospel and bring the reign of God to his staff,
ignores the leading of the Spirit and goes about
"Christianizing" his staff according to his own desires and
leadings.

The temptation to do it *our* way rather than God's is
common to all men. Satan fell from heaven and Adam and
Eve sinned because they thought they knew best. When
we seek to satisfy our own desires and pursue our own

plans, even in the "name of the Lord," we are like disobedient children playing in the flower garden when mother told us to stay on the lawn. We are doing what we want, not what is right.

This chapter examines a few of the pitfalls that the Christian manager must avoid in bringing the message of the Lord to the organization.

There is great danger in succumbing to one of these or a similar temptation. Any time we move out of the Lord's will when ministering to others, we are ministering according to our own imperfect wisdom. This means we are likely to be serving in such a way that we actually hinder the work of the Holy Spirit in the individual we are attending to. In a group setting like our staff, the receptiveness to Christ can be completely lost, at least for a time. If we want to build a Christ-centered organization, we must work to avoid errors that would tear down rather than build.

Six major problem areas will be considered briefly. The reader should note that in actual experience more than one of these problems can exist together, and can be mixed to varying degrees. The interrelatedness of these pitfalls is self-evident. They are:

1. The attitude that perceives the work place as a church.
2. The belief that all men must share the same spiritual experience.
3. Insistence that all men must be saved.
4. Emphasizing ministry to the detriment of work.
5. Handling all decisions and actions according to our desires without regard for God's direction.
6. Failure to make oneself available as an instrument

of God but relying exclusively on God to do the work without our actual cooperation.

The Work Place Is Not a Church

The true church, or body of Christ, is present in the work place whenever two or more Christians fellowship with one another in the Spirit, whether at lunch, coffee break, or in an off-hours Bible study. There is real danger when the manager or any of his staff begin to conceive of the work place fellowship as equivalent to, or in place of, the local congregation to which they belong.

This misconception arises when we reverse priorities and fail to understand that the primary reason for the organization's existence is to produce, not provide spiritual ministry or to save souls.

There is a place for ministry at work, but it must enhance and not interfere with the organization's primary mission. Even if there is regular group prayer and fellowship, the work place cannot and should not take the place of the local congregation, and the manager cannot take the place of an employee's pastor. While the two ministries are similar, they are predicated upon fundamentally different purposes and are not in competition with one another. Any ministry at work must complement that of the local church community and aid in the achievement of the organization's goals.

For example, the zealous, immature Christian may find himself with such a hunger for God that he spends large amounts of work time in prayer, Bible study, spiritual reading and discussions about his new-found enthusiasm. If the manager has fallen prey to the temptation to act primarily as a pastor he will encourage such a situation, possibly justifying it by shifting work assignments from his brother to others. If we pause to consider this situation we can see it is unhealthy for the organization, the particular employee and the manager. While the manager should encourage the person's spiritual growth and help to feed the spiritually hungry, he must understand that work cannot be put aside for that purpose and that, in fact, discipline in work is an important part of the Christian's growth.

If the manager becomes aware of such an attitude on his own or the staff's part, he must take immediate action to dispel it, even if it means the suspension of all fellowship and ministry activities until the proper balance can be obtained.

Everyone's Spiritual Experience Is Not the Same

One of the most effective ways to destroy existing fellowship and prevent new relationships from growing is to insist that all Christians must have the same spiritual experiences as defined by some authority, usually ourselves through the denominational doctrines to which we subscribe.

All men must submit to Jesus Christ as their Lord and confess Him as their Savior to receive salvation but the way this occurs for each individual is not the same. Furthermore, while the power flowing from the overflowing of the Spirit is available to all men, they do not have to experience it to become a Christian. Even those who are baptized in the Holy Spirit disagree about such matters as whether or not the gift of tongues should be manifested by all. The account of Cornelius's salvation experience and the Spirit baptism that was a part of it should be ample proof that we cannot prepackage or program the working of the Holy Spirit (Acts 10).

To insist on your doctrine rather than to focus on the lordship of Jesus Christ is to establish a barrier to the unity the Holy Spirit is calling us to. When we become human-centered by focusing on doctrine rather than truth, we harm the body of Christ. To fellowship in the unity of the Holy Spirit we must learn to lay down our doctrines, opinions and interpretations, and lift up Christ when we come together.

The manager must recognize that we are individuals and within the unity of the body the spiritual experiences of the believers are intensely personal. To share the things that have happened in our lives through the power of Christ is edifying provided we do not succumb to the religious temptation of making a doctrine of our experience. If we can maintain this perspective in our fellowship with one another we will be able to see our brethren in the unifying light of Christ rather than in the destructive, opinionated conceptions of man.

No Matter How Hard You Try, Not All Will Be Saved
We know God wills that all men be saved (1 Tim. 2:4). This is why He sent Jesus, but while salvation is available to all as a gift, not all will believe and accept it. To think our efforts of witness and ministry will bring all we come into contact with to salvation is a misunderstanding that can lead us to a busy and frivolous ministry. Yes, we are to make others aware of Christ, but we cannot force them to believe. Not everyone we share the good news with is going to accept it, no matter how hard we try to convince them. In fact, if we spend too much time badgering it might just be enough to convince others they are right in not believing. What we can do is to try to help them understand but we must remember that we cannot make

them understand. Like John the Baptist, we can help prepare the way of the Lord to a man's heart but we cannot convict a man of his sinfulness or convince him of his need for Christ.

Understanding this helps us to see why we may not be anointed to preach Jesus to everyone we meet and it helps us to learn to be sensitive to the Spirit's promptings as to when we should. For the Christian manager these opportunities will arise in the course of his work. We do not need to create or force them to happen. We need, rather, to be attentive to the Spirit's direction.

If we would all learn this, much misdirected and even injurious ministry could be avoided and the power and skills we possess for witness could be more effectively used.

Work Comes First

It must be emphasized again that the manager's first responsibility is to carry out the job he is paid for, to contribute to achieving the organization's objectives. Ministry should only be a complement to this. Whenever we minister to someone during working hours at least part of our objective should be to help that person perform his job better or to somehow improve the operations of the organization. If we counsel, teach, or minister without considering whether or not it has a place in our work, we are not doing what God wants us to do and we are not going to be effective witnesses. Being conformed to the will of God means doing what He says at every moment. When we have other work to do we are disobedient if we pursue a ministry.

Some Christian service will take place on company time but it should do something to contribute to the staff's effectiveness. Any that does not do this must be done during off hours and/or at break times. For example, when an employee is grieving because of death, divorce or some other traumatic loss, and this despondency is preventing him or her from doing the work assigned, it would be proper for the manager to counsel with and minister to the person through Scripture and prayer. This is certainly called for if the employee is to be encouraged to perform his or her job. On the other hand, the manager's priorities would be wrong if he took a staff member away from his machine or desk in order to preach Christ to him.

Do It God's Way

God's way will not necessarily be the easiest or most understandable to man, but His ways of operating are the most successful. When we fail to consult with the Lord and listen to what He wants us to do, we are being obedient to ourselves, not Him.

It is disastrous for man to get into a pattern of thinking that leads him to rely on his own wisdom. To do so is to deny that you need God and is a lack of trust in Him. Both are serious sins. Whenever man tries to govern or manage on his own strength he must be ready to pay the consequences for his mistakes.

The practical advice for the manager is: seek the direction of God in all that you do. Pray, asking for guidance and enlightenment. Search the Scriptures to know what God has already revealed that is applicable to the situation. Finally, counsel with not only the experts on your staff, but also with other discerning and mature Christians.

The degree to which we need to do these things will

vary according to the difficulty of the decision and the time available to consider it. Obviously, it would be foolish to spend three days praying and fasting, studying the Word and calling in counsel to decide whether to eliminate a report you believe to be nonessential. However, such a careful approach may be called for in deciding whether you should terminate an employee or enter into an expensive, somewhat uncertain, merger.

In either case, the principle is the same: seek the Lord on the matter. This may be in the form of a brief prayer such as, "Lord, help me in this decision" and then taking the action which seems best, or it may require something more rigorous like a retreat for several days where you can be alone with the Lord.

There is, however, another danger here that must also be addressed. That is, to seek God's direction can often be used as an excuse not to take action or to put off a needed decision. If this happens the manager is as equally remiss in his job and ministry as he is when failing to look for the path the Lord has prepared.

Thus, the manager must know how to hear the Lord's voice and to receive guidance, but he must also know how to act once he has received it. He must be spiritual but, as one brother has said, we must be careful not to become so spiritual that we are no earthly good.

We Are His Instruments

As we alluded to above, we cannot simply sit back and say, "I'll give it to God and let Him work it out." While it is true that we need to place all our problems, concerns, all of our life in God's hands so that He can direct us, we must recognize that often He uses us as instruments to "work it out." God never forces anything on us, not even His blessings. If we expect to receive we must learn to cooperate with Him.

When it comes to preaching the Word, God gives willing, open men the insight and the ability to do it. God is the source of the power—and men, by their willingness to serve, are the tools He uses. In like fashion, a Christian organization will not grow simply because the manager wants it and prays for it. He must first be willing to be used as a tool for the building of the kingdom.

As in the case of our office, Christ will not work among the staff unless there are those available who are willing to give up their own interests to help make Him known to others. Moses had to act so God would carry out the deliverance of the Israelites. Mary had to say yes to God and to bear the infant Christ for salvation to be born into the world. Someone needs to share Jesus with others, to provide opportunities for fellowship and study, before God will become incarnate in the organization.

This has been a very brief warning. Be aware of these and any other temptations that are marked by man's misconception of his role in God's plan and, often, by the tendency to be prideful or to put too much of self and not enough of Christ into the ministry. The best way of assuring that this does not happen is to be in tune with the Spirit, listen, pray and do it God's way and according to His schedule.

19

Bringing It Together

Blessed is the man who walks not in the counsel of the
wicked, nor stands in the way of sinners, nor sits in
the seat of scoffers; but his delight is in the law of the
Lord, and on his law he meditates day and night. He
is like a tree planted by streams of water, that yields
its fruit in its season, and its leaf does not wither. In
all that he does, he prospers. (Ps. 1:1-3)

The man who follows the Lord and lives by His Word is
blessed and bears much fruit. The man who relies on
himself and the ways of the world cannot be fruitful, for
there is no glory in man but that which God puts there.
This is the promise and the call of the Christian manager.
He is summoned to follow Jesus and to abide in the Word
of God that he may bear fruit for God in the organization
he manages. If he does these things he will be called
blessed and his is the promise of spiritual prosperity.

To be a Christian manager is to be a disciple who places
Christ first and relies on God's wisdom to guide him in a
pastoral ministry to the spiritual needs of his staff. Let us
reflect for a moment on what this means.

Discipleship

> And he said to all, "If any man would come after me,
> let him deny himself and take up his cross daily and
> follow me. For whoever would save his life will lose it;
> and whoever loses his life for my sake, he will save it.
> (Luke 9:23-24)

A manager must become a disciple before he can
minister. Until he becomes a disciple by emptying himself
for Christ he cannot be filled by God's grace to serve
others.

This is not an easy task. Christ was in agony as He bore
the cross and He asks each of us to "take up his cross."
There is no following Jesus without the pain of dying to
self, without the suffering of being cleansed of our
iniquity. When a man becomes a disciple, he is admitting,
"Lord, I am worthless. Do what you want with me. I
surrender my entire being to you."

The Primacy of Christ

> He is the head of the body, the church; he is the
> beginning, the first-born from the dead, that in
> everything he might be pre-eminent. (Col. 1:18)

Once submitted to Christ as a disciple we have begun to
recognize that He is first in all things. As a disciple we are
members of the body of which Jesus is head. To be a
Christian manager we must recognize and accept that this
headship extends to every area of our lives.

Empty of self, the Christian manager can serve as the
instrument God uses to manage the organization. If we do
not allow God to use us this way we are placing ourselves

in opposition to His headship and are placing ourselves in His position as a zealous radical might try to usurp a throne. We are lifting ourselves up as idols. When we are in opposition to God we are in conflict with Him, a conflict we cannot win and one which will never allow peace.

God's Wisdom

Let no one deceive himself. If any one among you thinks that he is wise in this age, let him become a fool that he may become wise. For the wisdom of this world is folly with God. For it is written, "He catches the wise in their craftiness," and again, "The Lord knows that the thoughts of the wise are futile." So let no one boast of men. (1 Cor. 3:18-21)

One way that the manager submits himself to God is by placing human wisdom in its proper perspective which is below the wisdom of God. The manager who relies primarily or solely on man's understanding to tell him how to meet the needs of his staff and handle people problems will not be able to resolve the matters with finality. In relying on God's wisdom as spoken through His Word, the manager is looking to the source of all answers. God's wisdom will bring about permanent solutions.

Pastoral Ministry

Tend the flock of God that is your charge, not by constraint but willingly, not for shameful gain but eagerly, not as domineering over those in your charge but being examples to the flock. (1 Pet. 5:2-3)

The Christian manager is also a minister. He relies on the Spirit of God to show him how to *serve* the staff. The world's concept of a manager is one who directs and leads others. This is certainly a part of the responsibility but the manager's ability to carry out these tasks must rest upon his reliance on God and desire to serve his staff by meeting their needs.

Spiritual Ministry

Above all hold unfailing your love for one another, since love covers a multitude of sins. Practice hospitality ungrudgingly to one another. As each has received a gift, employ it for one another, as good stewards of God's varied grace. (1 Pet. 4:8-10)

The secular manager can help to meet physical and emotional needs but cannot handle spiritual needs because he does not have the ability to recognize them or the desire to do anything if he understood them. As a minister, the Christian manager understands that the spirit is the real person and the most important part to minister to. Spiritual problems are often at the root of other problems and the resolution of spiritual difficulty must be the first step toward resolving those of other natures. The Christian manager is concerned with the whole man as God made him and not as man sees him.

A Summons To Ministry

We are called to the ministry God has prepared for us. If you are a manager, you are called to a ministry that revolves around that position. If you ignore the call, your decision will bear fruit like anxiety, confusion, inability to deal with problems, misdirection, lack of guidance and weakness. If you accept it, and eagerly receive God's anointing, you will bear the fruit of peace, joy, prosperity and all the good things our Father wants to give you.

The choice is yours to make but its effect goes beyond yourself. Not only your life but the lives of those you manage will be touched by your decision. This is the biggest decision you will face as a manager. God's way or man's way? What is your answer?

For free information on how to receive
the international magazine

LOGOS JOURNAL

also Book Catalog

Write: Information - LOGOS JOURNAL CATALOG
Box 191
Plainfield, NJ 07061